Prohibition's Second Failure

Prohibition's Second Failure

THE QUEST FOR A RATIONAL AND HUMANE DRUG POLICY

Theodore R. Vallance

PRAEGER

Westport, Connecticut
London

Library of Congress Cataloging-in-Publication Data

Vallance, Theodore R.
Prohibition's second failure : the quest for a rational and humane drug policy / Theodore R. Vallance.
p. cm.
Includes bibliographical references and index.
ISBN 0–275–94482–4 (alk. paper)
1. Drug abuse—Government policy—United States. 2. Narcotics, Control of—United States. 3. Drug legalization—United States.
I. Title.
HV5825.V32 1993
363.4′5′0973—dc20 92–35957

British Library Cataloguing in Publication Data is available.

Library of Congress Catalog Card Number: 92–35957
ISBN: 0–275–94482–4

First published in 1993

Praeger Publishers, 88 Post Road West, Westport, CT 06881
An imprint of Greenwood Publishing Group, Inc.

Printed in the United States of America

The paper used in this book complies with the Permanent Paper Standard issued by the National Information Standards Organization (Z39.48–1984).

10 9 8 7 6 5 4 3 2 1

Contents

Illustrations

FIGURE

TABLES

Preface

My interest in the problem of illicit drugs began twenty-five years ago when I was Chief of the Planning Branch at the National Institute of Mental Health (NIMH). At that time, NIMH had one program dealing with psychopharmacology and drug abuse, and another concerned with alcoholism. The Johnson administration's offensive against the drug problem (not then called a "war on drugs") was getting under way, and my organization's assignment was to develop budgetary recommendations for a few years, not only for NIMH (although that was our main focus) but with consideration as well for other federal agencies involved with the drug problem. A sizeable part of the tasks of data gathering and analysis was contracted to a consulting firm (Arthur D Little, Inc., as I remember) with the objective of coming up with some estimates of what the drug problem was costing the United States and what the government might have to spend to make a difference in that toll.

One of the most striking findings was that the illegality of using heroin, marijuana (cocaine was barely on the horizon, if at all visible), and some of the other hallucinogens generated costs—related to theft, rising insurance rates, police forces, courts, prisons, and lost productivity—that far exceeded the identifiable costs of treatment and other health-related matters. To us, these data suggested the possibility of easing up on the pursuit and prosecution of drug law offenders, and putting more money into efforts to treat existing drug abusers and to prevent others from joining their ranks. To no one's surprise, the Federal Bureau of Narcotics and other agencies and ancestors of today's war on drugs took unkindly to this idea. In all honesty, I cannot prove that these agencies even had a chance to make a formal review, for I recall that my superiors in the NIMH hierarchy reacted with horror at the prospect of doing battle with these agencies over a national program that might reduce their relative power and affluence. As a result, our "program analysis" (as planning documents were often called in those days) underwent a revision.

The last draft I know of, and of which I retain a copy, was a very respectable document whose focus remained within the Public Health Service. The document contained a historical review of the drug problem; and a description of extant programs of treatment, research, prevention, and training, plus plans to expand them over the subsequent five years. The document was assuredly no bombshell, but it did contain some little firecrackers.

An appendix to the NIMH document that analyzed the then-current legal structure and the possible aftereffects of alternatives also noted in brief tabular form the probable effects of keeping narcotics illegal and high-priced as compared with allowing them to become legal and low-priced. The estimated effects were quite in line with those projected by present-day reformers, but the report took no stand on legalization. The view expressed on marijuana control was distinctly positive as compared with today's official "establishment" view. The enforcement approach was said to obscure and distort the problem, and the document enumerated a goodly number of arguments favoring its regulation under the drug abuse control authority of the Food and Drug Administration. While recommending this approach to marijuana control, the document noted that the necessary "changes in federal legislation might well be opposed by the Federal Bureau of Narcotics." As you might imagine, this firecracker fizzled out.

As a note on the politics of government bureaucracies, it is interesting to observe in action the following principle: If you are in charge of a program dealing with a problem about which some potent segment of the public is concerned, get Congress to create a national institute for it. In the present instance, out of two relatively modest NIMH programs that dealt with increasingly visible public problems, there evolved two more national institutes within the Public Health Service: The National Institute on Drug Abuse and the National Institute on Alcohol and Alcohol Abuse. These institutions are now members of the second drug culture, which I describe in Chapter 1, complete with prestigious directorships, professional staffs, access to the upper levels of government, impressive budgets, and opportunities to do good.

As for this book: my approach is straightforward and simple—as simple, that is, as the huge literature on drug use, drug abuse, and the associated institutional arrangements and afflictions will allow. First, I will try to identify the problems that current drug programs—including the "war on drugs"—deal with, and to describe the contemporary context that influences how we respond to the problems. Then I examine the costs to society that the problems and the various "wars" against them create. Next comes an assessment of how well we are doing, including an attempt to clarify criteria by which such a judgment can be made. Then, recognizing the firmness with which federal policy seems committed to the criminalization approach, I look into the possible consequences of trying to keep on doing the same things but with more determination and money. Having concluded that more of the same would not give us relief from the most troublesome parts of the drug problem, I explore the other available options, and on the basis of that search came to a set of goals for a reformed drug policy and a package of policy proposals. Since no major change in national drug policy is likely to happen quickly or easily, I devote the final chapter to means toward reformist ends, hoping to make it easier for reform-minded people to take action beyond thinking earnestly that reform is sorely needed.

An additional comment on the literature is in order. As noted, it is truly colossal, its thousands of titles going far beyond the capacity of a lifetime's work to synthesize. For each citation in this book, there could easily be a dozen more to back it up—or, occasionally, to refute it. One of the best of the current books on drug policy reform has 162 pages of text, followed by 80 tightly packed pages of notes and references. For every major point in this and similar books, there is enough literature to support a book-length treatment. I have tried to avoid overloading the text with notes and asides, using enough citations, however, to lend credibility to major assertions and to provide the reader with sources useful in following up arguments.

My thanks go to several people who have been especially helpful in this enterprise. Primary among these is Professor Bruce Bullington, of Penn State's faculty of Administration of Justice. Bruce is a veritable walking encyclopedia on drug issues and has given unstintingly advice, documents, references, and the time to read and criticize the penultimate draft of the manuscript. Eric Sterling, President of the Criminal Justice Policy Foundation and all-around activist in the drug policy reform movement, also provided valuable review and criticism of parts of the draft and steered me to a number of documents and people who, in their own turns and ways, were helpful. The head of Penn State's program in Science, Technology, and Society, Dr. Carl Mitcham, provided financial help and clerical assistance to the project, embodied in the heads and hands of Betsy Held and Karen Hull. Associate Dean Stanley Mayers of the College of Health and Human Development also contributed encouragement and financial support. Melanie Romig's computer skills produced the index. My agent, Ruth Wreschner, deserves credit for promptly locating a quality publisher, and my editors improved on my prose in several places, spotted some potentially embarrassing errors, and needled me into adopting some niceties of form and notation that only an editor can love.

My wife Jean delivered a lot of good editorial criticism as well as help in proof reading and indexing, and put up with my obsession with the word processor and my absence from many (but not all) duties of household and garden. Love has been an indispensable asset throughout the project.

Finally, of course, I absolve all of these good people of responsibility for the book's errors and omissions, reserving same for myself.

Prohibition's Second Failure

Chapter 1

Defining Today's Drug Problem in the United States

Practically no one will disagree that America has a serious problem with illicit drugs that is very complicated and has several interrelated aspects. As a public health problem, the use of illicit drugs exacts high costs in dollars for treatment and in reduced quality of individual and family life. As a problem of law enforcement, drug use demands ever-higher dollar costs through arrests, prosecution, and jailing, not to mention the costs of trying to foil the importation of drugs. As a political problem, illicit drug use and people's fears about drugs have made it risky in the extreme for politicians to go beyond recommending changes in local marijuana laws even to suggest a general tempering of our hard-line "war" on drugs. And as a general social problem, illicit drug use is connected with uncountable costs in broken homes, deteriorating neighborhoods, failing schools, and infringements of civil liberties.

In addition to its relatively imaginable aspects, the illicit drug problem has produced a continuing set of opportunity costs—that is, the costs of lost opportunities to use money that has been consumed by efforts to cope with the drug problem and that might instead have been used for purposes that could enhance the quality of our individual lives and of our society as a whole.

It is salutary that many thoughtful people, mostly but not entirely outside of government, are raising questions about the value of many aspects of our policies on illicit drugs. Notably, the Drug Policy Foundation, the National Organization for the Reform of Marijuana Laws (NORML), and the National Drug Strategy Network, all in Washington, D.C., have developed and promoted the spread of useful information with which to examine the many aspects of our policy on illicit drugs. Academics nationwide are analyzing and debating the issue. *The Journal of Drug Issues* is but one regular publication presenting various aspects of the problem. In addition to NORML's many local chapters, several grass-roots organizations such as the Religious Coalition for a Moral Drug Policy are also working toward a better understanding of, and solutions for, the drug problem. Even people thought of as political and economic conservatives, such as former Secretary of State George Schultz,[1] essayist-publisher William F. Buckley, and Nobel Prize economist Milton Friedman,[2] are making the case for legalizing the use of now illegal drugs.

In this book, I argue for an evolution of our drug policy in the direction of reducing the harms associated with drugs and increasing the opportunities for constructive personal and social development. Right now I want to clarify my aims by noting two major harms related to the drug problem: (1) there is the biological and psychological harm connected with the excessive use—abuse—of drugs, in this context the illicit drugs; (2) there is the harm inflicted on individuals and on our social institutions—the family, schools, and the justice system particularly—by the immense effort to stamp out all use of illicit drugs represented by the war on drugs. I shall argue for a gradual and general withdrawal from that war, but with the understanding that the first and principal promise of "decriminalization," or even legalization, will be to reduce drug-related crime and its tremendous costs and terrors. The problem of abusing drugs will not be quickly solved by relaxing the criminalization of drug trafficking and use. However, solution of that problem can be materially accelerated by wisely using the resources of people and money redirected from the "war" in ways that can reduce people's needs for excessive drug use.

In the next chapter, I will show in some detail the high costs of the drug problem—in dollar and non-dollar terms. Chapter 3 assesses the progress in the drug wars thus far. Chapter 4 surveys the options that are available to cope with the drug problem under the present policy of prohibition. It will become evident that the options for evolving a new national drug policy are risky, difficult to attain, and necessary. In the final three chapters, I analyze still other alternative policy orientations and propose a new policy and steps toward establishing it.

THE NEED FOR A NATIONAL POLICY ON DRUGS

It is an innate characteristic of humans to seek pleasure and to invent more effective and efficient ways of producing it. Fortunately for the world's historical and cultural heritages, human pleasure seeking has produced what people value—the arts, the architecture, the literature and the sciences of the great civilizations, and the machines and organizations that create and distribute goods that people need and want. We can be ever grateful that people can find joy in creative activities.

Some forms of pleasure seeking are less productive than others, but still have legitimate places in the operation of a civilized society. I think of the passive "addictions," over the centuries, of gladiators striving to kill one another or football players scrambling to beat an opposing team through application of greater weight and force. The performers can enjoy the thrills of accomplishment and the rewards of income, and, for half of the gladiators, the prospect of fame in another encounter. But the thrill-seeking spectator produces little beyond injecting into the sports economy a few dollars for tickets, beer, hot dogs, or souvenirs.

Among the earliest enhancers of pleasure has been alcohol, first in the form of wine, then beer, then distillates. A gentle combination of food, drugs, and sex was described in the twelfth century by Omar:

> Here with a loaf of bread beneath the bough
> A flask of wine, a loaf of bread, and thou
> Beside me singing in the wilderness
> And wilderness is paradise enow.

Some eight hundred years later a similar thought was expressed by an unknown poet imitating the style of Ogden Nash:

> Wine and bread beneath the bough
> Engender warmth and lovers' vow
> But if you want to be adventurous
> With whiskey you become licenturous.[3]

The concern of a national drug policy is the management of chemical inducers of mood changes or relievers of pain and grief. The United States does not have a uniform policy on drugs. Indeed the use of nicotine, alcohol, caffeine, and the legally available psychoactive prescription drugs (tranquilizers, sedatives, anti-depressants) is variously discouraged and encouraged through sundry public policies. We have these drugs, we tolerate them, and we try rather haphazardly to control them.

Our overall drug policy (if it is correct to say that we have one) is truly a mixed bag of compromises among numerous interests in our pluralistic democracy. The Surgeon General warns of the hazards of tobacco smoking, and Congress legislates warning labels on cigarettes; however, the Department of Agriculture subsidizes the growing of tobacco. The National Institute of Alcohol and Alcohol Abuse (NIAAA) seeks to ameliorate the effects of alcohol—our most expensively abused drug—and Congress grants tax deductions as a legitimate business expense for advertising alcoholic drinks. The states, through taxes and state-owned liquor stores, enjoy the revenues and profits from the sale of "booze" while paying out millions for treating alcoholics and prosecuting people for driving under the influence (DUI). As a general guide to human welfare, it can be argued that substances—licit or illicit—that induce thrills or relieve momentary distress are not among the more acceptable aids to human development in the long run.

Sorely needed is a uniform and consistent national orientation toward substances that, when ingested, change moods or significantly impact on internal bodily functions and that can produce harm when over-used. Our present loose orientation permits and even encourages—though it does not expressly condone or advocate—the use of some harmful drugs to excess while sternly forbidding even the possession of others. The mixed message results in cynicism about political institutions and sets a model that encourages the compromising of principles supporting long-term public good in the interest of short-term expediency.

Historical Perspective

A brief history of American drug policy might be helpful in setting the stage for what follows. Until the latter part of the nineteenth century, government policy was libertarian and hands-offish. Drugs were generally seen as beneficent medicines until the last quarter of the century when the addictive properties of morphine, long a favorite pain reliever, became evident and troublesome. The stimulating properties of cocaine were also well known, and the drug was included in Coca-Cola until 1903. In 1906 the Pure Food and Drug Act required identification of all medicinal ingredients on product labels, and physicians began to cut down on the use of morphine.

The first major federal drug law was the Harrison Act of 1914, which regulated opiates and cocaine through record-keeping rules and taxation. Interestingly, this act was passed partly to show the Chinese that we were serious about our urging other nations to reduce trade in narcotics and partly to assist the Chinese, who also wanted other nations to exercise more control over drug traffic as a part of their own long struggle with the abuses of opium. Although written as a taxation measure, the Harrison Act was clearly intended by the enforcement agencies to prohibit the use of cocaine and narcotic drugs, to remove such drugs totally from non-medical commerce, and to prevent physicians and pharmacists from supplying users with drugs when no medical treatment was intended.[4] Regulated medical uses of morphine and cocaine continued through the 1920s, though general imports of these drugs for other than medical uses were banned.

In 1930 the Federal Bureau of Narcotics (FBN) was established in the Treasury Department, and a crusading anti-drug activist, Harry J. Anslinger, was named director. From then on, the medical orientation toward the drug problem was subordinated in federal policy to the criminal one. Anslinger, who remained FBN Director until 1962, sparked increasingly punitive laws against drugs, beginning with the Marijuana Tax Act of 1937 which, as the Harrison Act did for narcotics and cocaine, restricted marijuana's use to a very few medical processes, imposed taxes on its importation, and made unauthorized possession a criminal act. The hardening of popular opinion against any use of illicit drugs was aided by Anslinger's many speeches and writings and by popular motion pictures such as *Reefer Madness*, which protrayed marijuana as a grotesque and horrible presence in society.

Additional laws in the fifties further tightened criminal sanctions against the possession, trade, and use of marijuana, cocaine, and heroin; the death penalty was authorized for a person over 18 convicted of selling heroin to a minor.

The first heavy assault, if not a full blown "war" on drugs began in the 1960s with the Johnson administration. In 1968, the old Bureau of Narcotics was merged with the Bureau of Drug Abuse Control from the Department of Health, Education, and Welfare into a new Bureau of Narcotics and Dangerous Drugs (BNDD), assigned to the Justice Department and given broader enforcement powers. Contemporaneously, the medical orientation began to reappear, with the rise of new treatment methods and an increased recognition of the drug problem as one of public health. Nonetheless, the laws and their sanctions remained in full force. This war was accelerated in the Nixon administration through the Comprehensive Drug Abuse Prevention and Control Act of 1970. Though originally intended to consolidate drug-related legislation written over the preceding sixty years, the act ended up with major revisions to penalties for violations and strengthened regulation of the pharmaceutical industry. Its Title II, the Controlled Substances Act, established five separate categories, or "schedules," for classifying and regulating narcotics and other dangerous drugs.

The five schedules now encompass more than twenty thousand substances, ranging from those judged most harmful and likely to be abused, to relatively benign, palliative drugs. In reading these schedules, it is useful to keep in mind that they represent a mixture of attitudes and fears, some scientific knowledge, plus political agendas of the government agencies that produced them. The schedules are essentially compromises reached between Senate and House committees and their Democratic and Republican legislators, and between Congress and the Nixon administration. Still worse, the act authorized the attorney general (not the surgeon general) to alter the classifications from time to time as needed. Judges found themselves bound by this political, not scientific, classification system in assessing penalties, and drug education programs still take cues from it.[5]

The terms *medicinal use*, *addictive potential*, and *abuse* are ill-defined even twenty-some years after the schedules were created. As a single example, marijuana, located in Schedule I, is now known to have next to no potential for addiction and to have some genuinely—even if not dramatically—positive medical uses, but it remains in Schedule I. The classification system and the way it is used today are examples of what Erich Goode has called "the politics of reality."[6] In this process, reality and truth become established on the basis of repeated statements by people in high positions or having technical or scientific credibility.

- Schedule I includes drugs with no accepted medicinal use in the United States and having high probability for abuse: heroin, LSD, marijuana, peyote, mescaline, psylocibin, methaqualone, cocaine. For a first offense, possession of 10 grams of LSD or 50 grams of cocaine with intent to distribute can produce sentences of twenty years to life and fines of one to five million dollars.
- Schedule II includes drugs with high probability of abuse and causative of severe dependence: opium, morphine, codeine, methadone, methamphetamine. These have medicinal use under close supervision. Penalties for violation are the same as for Schedule I drugs.

Schedule I and II drugs are most relevant to the war on drugs, but for comparison, here is the rest of the list:

- Schedule III includes drugs with lesser probability of abuse, such as paregoric (containing opium), and available only by prescription.
- Schedule IV includes drugs with lesser probability of abuse than those in Schedule III, such as barbiturates and diazepam (Valium), and sleeping pills, available by prescription.

- Schedule V includes drugs with still less likelihood of abuse, containing minute amounts of opium or codeine, such as cough medicines or compounds to control diarrhea. Illegal trafficking in these can bring fines of $100,000 to $250,000 and prison terms of up to a year.

In 1973 President Nixon ordered the creation of the Drug Enforcement Administration (DEA) with the mission to immobilize by arrest and prosecution major drug violators to the Controlled Substances Act operating at interstate and international levels. The DEA took over the Customs Service's Drug Intelligence Unit, the old BNDD, the Office of National Narcotics Intelligence, and the Office of Drug Abuse Law Enforcement. Without dwelling on the details of these bureaucratic arrangements, it is possible to take note of them to illustrate a growing tendency toward the assumption of power into a national drug police force, in contrast to traditional state and local authority, a force whose power has continued to expand to this day.

The Ford and Carter administrations were less consumed by the drug problem, with President Carter going so far as to suggest that the mere possession of a small amount of marijuana be decriminalized. Carter believed that police resources could be better used against the "hard" drugs and more serious crime. Neither administration, however, made any moves against the existing body of anti-drug law.

The second and fully declared war on drugs began in the Reagan years and has been expanded with increased budgets and stronger rhetoric during the Bush administration. In 1982 the attorney general reorganized the Department of Justice so that the Drug Enforcement Administration director was responsible to the Director of the Federal Bureau of Investigation. Enforcement was increased; the Posse Comitatus Act, proscribing the use of the military in enforcing domestic laws, was revised in 1982 to permit military interdiction of inward-bound drugs,[7] and again in 1986 to provide for emergency assistance to civilian law enforcement agencies.[8] A major new Anti-Drug Abuse Act was passed in 1986, which among other things expanded various penalties and extended the Drug-Free Schools and Communities Act to apply to colleges and universities. Punishments were made more severe, such as providing a mandatory minimum $1,000 fine for a first offense of possessing any amount of any illegal drug, and 15 days in jail and a $2500 fine for a second offense. (Appendix A contains a summary of major federal drug laws.) The DEA has become a very large outfit, with well over 5,000 people in its employ, including around 3,000 special agents, nearly 600 lawyers, 200 intelligence specialists, 150 or so chemists, and many other specialists. It has offices in several countries, notably Bolivia, Peru, Mexico, France, Thailand, Turkey, and Colombia, and a proposed 1992 appropriation of $748 million.

A diagrammatic summary of this history is shown in Figure 1.1, adapted from a 1990 report by the Institute of Medicine, "Treating Drug Problems."[9] A compilation of major current federal drug laws appears in Appendix A. Their very number suggests how complicated the law on drugs has become, and how much interest legislators running for re-election have had in associating themselves with the war on drugs.

Against this brief historical background, and with growing suspicion among students of drug policy that the war on drugs as presently being conceived and conducted may not be finally winnable, let's examine some features of the drug problem and the war on drugs and their setting within contemporary society.

HOW DRUG DEPENDENT ARE WE?

A little reflection on the content of the commercials shown in an evening's TV viewing will suggest the ease with which Americans turn to drugs to relieve pain or enhance pleasure or comfort: Have trouble falling to sleep? Use Sominex or Sleep-Eze. (Don't try to figure out why you can't sleep. Just take a pill.) Head aches? Try Bayer's or Tylenol. (Forget about what stresses may be bothering you. Just take a pill.) Overheated from mowing the lawn? Relax with a cool Bud, or Stroh's, or Miller's. (Water? Perish the thought!) Constipated? Go for that good old MOM. (Just take a pill. Never mind a high fiber diet!) Hemorrhoids? There's always Preparation H (changing the way you eat or having surgery is a real pain.) Stomach gas? Go for that Pepto-Bismol or Tums. (Change your diet? Forget it!) Hangover? Reach for the Alka-Seltzer. (Cut down on alcohol? No way. Enjoy yourself and wipe out the after-effects with a pill). Other products come readily to mind but I trust the point is clear: We are encouraged to use drugs casually to relieve symptoms of problems that could be solved or prevented by attending to their causes.

What about prescription-controlled drugs? A 1979 book entitled *The Tranquilizing of America*[10] reported on psychoactive (mood-changing) prescription drugs. More than 57 million prescriptions of Valium resulted in 3.2 billion pills being taken; an estimated 900 people died using them. About twelve-and-three-quarter million prescriptions were issued for a little over 400 million sleeping pills with the brand name Dalmane; 100 people died using this drug. And for people who felt depressed, there were nearly nine million prescriptions for 588 million pills of Elavil to make

Figure 1.1
A Simplified Spectrum of Governing Ideas About Drugs*

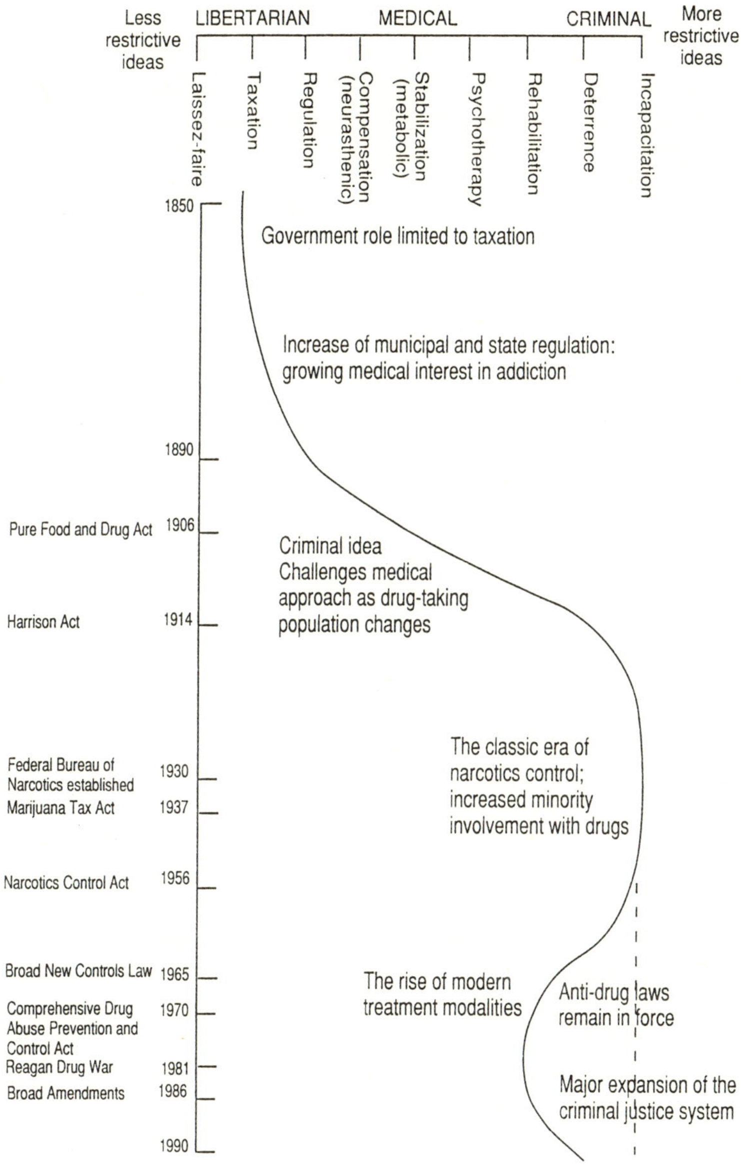

*Adapted from Institute of Medicine, 1990.

them feel better; about 700 people died. (These death estimates include uses of the drugs alone or in combination with others.)

Yes, we are a society that values the quick fix, that does not like to wait for solutions that may erase the cause of the problem but take more time. And our willingness to lean on mood-changing drugs—whether over-the-counter or by prescription—is one sign of this impatience. Equally obvious and far more tragic is the use of cocaine or heroin to escape depression or to find the happiness that is normally connected with rewarding work or wholesome family life.

THREE DRUG CULTURES

The term *culture* is commonly used to stand for the pattern of attitudes, values, beliefs, and behaviors that identify a particular cluster of people; by providing norms, the pattern helps people to define themselves and maintain their existence as a group. It is a loose term, and no one can claim a final or official definition, but it is often useful in describing social problems. Before identifying the three contemporary drug cultures, it will be instructive to consider North American class structure and take a look at history to see the class-and-drug connection.

An important but not clearly understood aspect of the drug problem derives from its being entwined with differences in socio-economic classes in the United States. Despite proclamations about being an open society and exhortations to believe that the American dream can be eventually realized by anyone willing to work hard, we have always had an underclass of the unemployed, underemployed, and undereducated for whom entry to the middle class is an exceedingly low probability. That this large underclass exists and that negative attitudes about it are held by the middle and upper classes are partly responsible for the ferocity with which the drug war is waged. It is not difficult for many who make up the middle and upper classes to think of people who are poor or afflicted by economic and racial sterotypes as somehow qualitatively different and resigned to bearing the burdens of well-intended anti-drug laws that turn out to have repressive consequences for these people—who happen neither to vote in large numbers nor to lobby their legislators. John Helmer's book *Drugs and Minority Oppression*[11] analyzes in detail the connection between the drug war and class conflict.

Historically, the Chinese in California were the first to be stigmatized in the context of drug use and abuse. I simplify Helmer's account to make the point. As the California economy rapidly expanded in the years just after the gold rush, Chinese immigration was encouraged in order to fill the demand for cheap labor. After 1852 the Chinese came in increasing numbers and filled not only the demands for a grunt labor force but entered entrepreneurial roles in commerce. As the gold fields played out in about 1863, the Chinese became part of a serious labor surplus. One use of this surplus was the hiring by the Central Pacific Railroad, later by other railroads, of large numbers of Chinese to break strikes of white workers. This laid the basis for anti-Chinese agitation, though not much of this occurred immediately. It was later in the 1870s when competition from goods manufactured on the East Coast, competition made possible by the completion of the railroads, led to a general slump in the California manufacturing economy. Chinese businessmen, seeking to maintain their way of living, imported ever-larger amounts of smokeable opium and succeeded in marketing it widely, mainly to Chinese, who used it as a medium of exchange for goods and services as well as for pleasure.

The economic prosperity and visibility of the Chinese made it easy for whites to become antagonistic. The first anti-drug law in the country, passed as a San Francisco ordinance in 1875, prohibited the smoking of opium and the operation of "dens" for that purpose. The ordinance said next to nothing about the drug or its possible bad effects. As Helmer observes:

> That the antiopium laws were put into operation, and that notions about the drug being harmful and dangerous, were expressed and eventually believed is indicative of a class ideology in the making. . . . The principal factor involved was the existence of a labor market split less by skill or the characteristics of industrial organization than by race, for the latter, much more than the former, set the pattern for determining wages.[12]

Helmer goes on to analyze the situation of Mexican-American laborers and poorly paid urban blacks and whites in much the same vein. He argues throughout that the power of the drug mythology, particularly the assertion that addiction is an inevitable outcome of drug use and that the addict can neither control nor stop consumption, which impels him to irrational extremes of behavior, finds its power "as motivation and rationalization for the methods used to settle economic conflict and put down the popular unrest that has caused the conflict."[13] Helmer does not attribute this condition to conscious conspiracy, but sees it as the natural, if unplanned, outcome of the maintenance of power by the powerful.

The Culture of Users and Dealers

The most commonly imagined modern day "drug culture" is thought to be made up mostly of youngish, erratically employed people who use or exchange drugs regularly, sell drugs to whomever they safely can, know people like themselves reasonably well, support one another in their belief that their connection with drugs and the life outside the law is okay, and do not trust strangers, who they think might set the police on them. The term "drug culture" was coined in the 1960s and '70s when heroin was gaining salience as a drug problem, and marijuana, LSD, and other psychedelic and mood-altering drugs were prominently used by college-age people, making up the "hippie" drug-using culture.

A related, more urbanized drug culture, based on heroin and the newly available cocaine, appeared slightly later. This drug culture, operating on solid capitalist principles, definitely still exists, and is exemplified eloquently in Terry Williams's book *The Cocaine Kids*.[14] Williams portrays the lives of these young people as they conduct their drug business in ways similar to other businesses: recruiting customers, keeping them happy, ensuring a steady supply and suitable quality of product, keeping eyes on colleagues and competitors, and maximizing their returns, all the while aspiring to get out of the drug business and into the legitimate economy after making a lot of "crazy money." This drug culture also includes, of course, the dealers and traffickers well above the street level, and the producers of the marketable product. It is a hectic and dangerous culture, but a working culture nonetheless.

It is important to note, however, that neither drug cultures of the sort that Williams portrays nor the stereotypical drug culture of "hippies" and other countercultural groups can describe the greatest number of users or even abusers. According to research summarized by Richard Miller, most drug users are occasional, moderate, or even steady users, people who carry on productive lives not at all dedicated—"addicted"—to the daily pursuit of drugs and whose drug use does not harm other people.[15] And yet, it is these people, mostly productive and law-abiding citizens, who are seen in the Office of National Drug Control Policy (ONDCP) as the main enemy in the drug war. The ONDCP's publication, *National Drug Control Strategy*, makes this clear, as will be shown shortly.

The Drug War–Dependent Culture

A second and much more powerful drug culture, which also supports well the lives of its members, is the set of organizations committed to reducing either the activity or the effects of the first drug culture. The rhetoric usually calls for stamping out the first drug culture or ameliorating its bad consequences, but without it the second would have no raison d'être. As noted earlier, the Drug Enforcement Administration alone has over five thousand employees. To my knowledge, no accounting has been rendered of the number of people occupied in other aspects of law enforcement, prosecution, and imprisonment of offenders, or of the numbers engaged in interdicting shipments bound our way and in helping various Latin American governments deal with our drug problem. And we should not forget the other people who live well on this drug-dependent culture: trial lawyers, prosecutors and assistant prosecutors, academics, columnists, publicists, talk-show hosts, miscellaneous court employees, and probation officers. Then there is the treatment community of individual psychiatrists, psychologists, and counselors of various ilks, hospitals, clinics, residential treatment communities, and the insurance companies who pay them, all conscientiously committed to doing their part in coping with the national drug problem. Finally, there are the drug-use testing and security industries whose profitability depends significantly on the continuing drug problem; by 1987, revenues of the drug-testing industry had grown to more than $100,000,000 and, by this writing, are probably closer to a billion dollars annually.[16] The interests, beliefs, attitudes, values, norms, and behaviors (not to mention mere practical things like careers) of a lot of people make up this particular drug culture.

The Culture of Legal Drugs

The third drug culture is broader and more heterogeneous and includes a very large proportion of the U.S. population: those who only use legal recreational drugs—alcohol and nicotine, over-the-counter treatment drugs such as aspirin, ibuprofen, milk of magnesia, and so on, and hundreds of prescription drugs, plus their manufacturers, sellers, advertising agencies, and communications media. These people, like participants in the other drug cultures, live better as a result of their participation in this drug culture—with the important exception of the 400,000 people who die each year as a result of nicotine addiction, the nearly 35,000 who die annually from alcohol-related illnesses,[17] and the many thousands developing criminal records and serving time for "driving under the influence," violent assault, and other outcomes of excessive alcoholic recreation. One of the normative attitudes of this culture is that it is bad for many reasons to use the illegals to solve problems or to feel good. Another attitude is that it is good to use legal drugs, however dangerous some of them might be, for the same purposes. Still another is that "we are not in any way like that bunch of depraved addicts and pushers that is causing all the trouble."

It is this large and powerful drug culture that sustains our hypocritical policy toward drugs in general. It is this same drug culture that makes so difficult any effort to change public attitudes toward the illegals, to inform the public about the hazards—to health, the economy, and democratic institutions and processes—that our present policy and its pursuits virtually guarantee.

ILLICIT DRUGS

Now we turn to a closer look at illicit drugs. The need to feel good and the cultural permission to use legal recreational and medical drugs, represented by our nearly unquestioning willingness to reach for the booze in the bottle and the palliative in the pharmacy, are easily stretched to include use of the illegal drug and its promise of relief from stress or of new and exciting experiences. Especially if there is little in our daily lives to feel good about, and if the prospect is poor for having productive work that leads to good feelings about ourselves, the temptation of the quick drug fix looms large. And if the quick fix promptly produces quick relief from pain and fear or generates a really terrific high, a lot of people will take more and more to the so-called hard drugs like heroin or the various forms of cocaine. Marijuana is also a mood modifier and is equally unlawful most places; however, it is quite unlike the others in its effects on behavior and health.

The phrase "national drug problem" commonly refers to only some of what I have mentioned so far. We are not yet in the habit of thinking of over-the-counter and prescription drugs as part of a "drug problem." They are simply a part of our culture. Ditto with caffeine, for which little harm is widely reported. Alcohol and nicotine? Yes, they are clearly health problems—the worst drug-related health problems we have—but we do not worry greatly about them until someone we love is killed in a DUI incident or dies of lung cancer. The substances are not illegal and hence not targets of moral condemnation, nor are they the subject of shoot-outs and jailings, like "real" or "hard" drugs. The hard drugs are what get political rhetoric and public opinion worked up from time to time, impressed as we are with the tragedy of drug-dominated neighborhoods, the skill of a big police drug bust, or the thrill of a street chase in a movie or on television.

Let us briefly examine the extent of the drug problem. First, it is a hot political potato. People nation-wide believe in the seriousness and existence of it. Politicians and publicists thrive on that belief. According to a report from the Bureau of Justice Statistics, the proportion of the public believing that drug abuse is the "most serious problem facing our country" rose from 2 percent in January 1985 to 27 percent in May 1989.[18] Still bigger proportions believe that drug abuse is a "very serious" problem. One can reasonably question whether these reported public judgments are based on conscientious reading of the day-to-day news about the drug problem or on the repeated assertions by public figures, law enforcement people, or other members of the second drug culture telling the public about the problem. The self-sustaining capacities of bureaucracies should never be underestimated. Eliot Abrams, former Assistant Secretary of State for Latin American Affairs, has said that "attacking the traffic in narcotics is as high a priority as we have in the U.S. government."[19] Presidents Nixon and Bush have referred to drug abuse as public enemy number one. Mr. Bush's secretary of state and chief of staff, James Baker III, has said of the drug problem, "There is no foreign policy issue short of war or peace which has a more direct bearing on the well-being of the American people."[20] Can lesser politicians afford to "look soft" on drugs?

Second, millions of people do use illicit drugs, many of them quite often, and a great many more occasionally. We probably have around 500,000 heroin users in various degrees of dependency.[21] Of high school seniors anonymously surveyed in 1988, 18 percent reported having used marijuana in the past thirty days, 33 percent in the past year.[22] A 1988 household survey conducted anonymously for the National Institute on Drug Abuse produced estimates that about twenty-two million citizens used cocaine in some form at least once, with about 5.8 million using it monthly.[23]

The actual use of marijuana and cocaine exceeds these survey-based estimates by an unknown but surely large margin, partly because the surveys do not sample the millions of high school drop-outs and homeless people. Both of these groups are far more likely to use illicit drugs than the population actually sampled. Further error is built into the household surveys by their omission of military personnel and people living in hospitals, dormitories, and prisons. Finally, under-use estimates are virtually guaranteed by the setting in which the questions are asked: given the potentially serious consequences of admitting to having used an illegal drug, many users—regular or occasional—will remain suspicious of any assurances of anonymity that may accompany the interview or questionnaire. Cocaine-related hospital emergencies are reported in an upward trend through the middle to late 1980s, though this trend has shown signs of slowing in more recent years.[24]

As a preview to the economic side of the drug problem, it can be noted that marijuana, considered a lesser health risk than other drugs because it is normally smoked rather than taken intravenously with dirty needles or contaminated by impure dilutants, accounted in the mid-80s for sales of about $14 billion (untaxed) dollars at the street level; this does not take into account the (also untaxed) sales between producers and distributors at various other levels.[25] A report from the Office of National Drug Control Policy estimates 1990 expenditures by American consumers of $18 billion for cocaine, $12 billion for heroin, and $8.3 billion for marijuana (down from the report cited earlier).[26] Although dedicated drug warriors may decry these figures as representing total losses to the economy, such a claim is unwarranted: the people receiving the payments do not drop the money into a hole, but put it instead into consumer goods, real estate, investments or to other constructive and taxable uses.

Further statistics on the use of illicit drugs abound, and horror stories of the ravages that are inflicted on individual lives by drugs and the conditions in which they are most frequently used can be found in the popular media almost daily.

A third feature of the drug problem is the continued injustice in the enforcement of the laws to control it. The burden falls disproportionately on the poor and powerless. A recent book by Clarence Lusane extends Helmer's 1975 analysis of drugs and minorities, and reports a disquieting number of facts that emphasize the misfortune of being born with socially built-in racial and economic disadvantages.[27] With the growing concern over fetal endangerment from mothers' drug use, women in general are exposed to the risk of being charged with drug offenses. Physicians in Florida tend to turn in black women who test positive for drugs at a rate ten times greater than that for white women who do.[28] Lusane describes a 1988 District of Columbia case of a pregnant woman who received the unusually long jail sentence of 180 days after pleading guilty to forging $700 in checks. The sentencing judge candidly admitted his intention of protecting the unborn child from the consequences of the mother's dependence on cocaine, even though drug use in the district's jails is common.

Surveys by the National Institute on Drug Abuse (NIDA) do not reflect disproportionate numbers of African Americans and Latinos using illicit drugs, but in 1989 blacks represented 41 percent of people arrested on drug charges:

The drug crisis in the Black community has been labelled by some analysts as "chemical warfare" against Black people. Blacks make up 50 percent of those admitted to emergency rooms for heroin, 55 percent of those for cocaine, and 60 percent of those for PCP. Blacks comprised 31 percent of all people with drug emergencies in 1985 and 25 percent of those in treatment for drugs in 1987.[29]

This situation fits with Andrew Hacker's recent, more general analysis of the disadvantages of not being born white in America. Hacker attends to the causes and effects of the persistence of inequality, reporting that nearly half of black children and about 16 percent of white children live below the government's "official" poverty line, and that black college men earn only slightly more than white men who only graduated from high school. Specifically bearing on the drug problem, he reports that nearly 42 percent of drug-related arrests are of African Americans—well over three times their proportion of the population. No believer in conspiracy theories, Hacker concludes that the reason for the grim picture of *Two Nations: Blacks, White, Separate, Hostile, Unequal* rests

> with a past that has shaped our present, and a present that makes use of the past. Race has made America its prisoner since the first chattels were landed on these shores. . . . A nation that has done so much to stress racial divisions should not be surprised if the result is not compassion and fellow feeling, but withdrawal and recrimination.[30]

As I type these words, there are more than forty fires burning in Los Angeles as blacks express their outrage over the acquittal by an all-white jury of four white Los Angeles police officers charged with using excessive force in the billy-club beating of black motorist Rodney King as he lay on the ground after being stopped for speeding and resisting arrest. The fires, the verdict, and the beating's videotape summarize Hacker's message of tragedy and injustice more vividly than words possibly can.

With opportunities for the good life virtually foreclosed for large numbers of minorities and poor citizens, can we wonder that we have a problem coping with substances to which millions of people may turn for momentary relief from the drudgery and hopelessness of their days?

THE ESTABLISHMENT VIEWPOINT

To describe further the context of official drug policy, it will be helpful to make special note of a document central to that policy, *The National*

Drug Control Strategy, especially its first edition of 1989.[31] The document was issued by the Office of National Drug Control Policy of which William Bennett was the first director and "drug czar." This document is the epitome of what Zimring and Hawkins call a legalist manifesto.[32] To the label of legalist I would add moralist, for the document not only emphasizes the illegality of owning, using, selling or in general having anything to do with illicit drugs, but stresses how downright bad these activities are and how inherently bad the drugs themselves are.

The National Drug Control Strategy has a number of interesting features. First, it asserts that the essence of the drug problem is "use itself" and that highest priority should be given to attacking use nation-wide—experimental first use, casual use, regular use, and addictive use alike. The focus of the attack should be not on addicts but on the millions of non-addicted drug users, each of whom is "highly contagious" and a potential "agent of infection."

Second, the document treats all drugs, illegal ones, that is, as equally pernicious, and nowhere suggests a choice of priorities among drugs in allocating resources for waging a war on drugs. To reduce the overall level of drug use nation-wide is declared as the highest priority. Thus, all drugs are similar to one another and bear no resemblance to legal drugs.

Third, the effort to control drugs appears essentially as a battle between good and evil. "Drug use is a moral problem," according to the document, which finds a neat dichotomy in the country: drug use and drug users that represent the forces of evil, versus "the vast majority of Americans who have never taken an illegal drug" and, of course, their government, representing the forces of good.

Fourth, like most documents written by committees or "offices," it contains some interesting inconsistencies. While asserting that all (illegal) drugs are created equal, the *National Drug Control Strategy* says that "crack" cocaine is the most dangerous and quickly addictive drug known; it also says that marijuana should be prohibited because it is a "gateway" drug leading to the use of more dangerous ones; thus, cocaine is the most dangerous drug in the world, and marijuana is just as bad.

All of these features betoken the legalistic-moralistic thrust of the *National Drug Control Strategy* and support the conclusion, rather frightening in my view, that the essence of current official policy is simply, and only, to uphold and enforce the law in all aspects and as it now stands. Public health and other arguments around the consequences of different uses of different drugs by different parts of the population are irrelevant, and according to Zimring and Hawkins:

The reason that decriminalization of any currently illegal drug is anathema to the legalist position is that the vindication of state authority is the central value to be upheld in this version of the drug war. Changing the law would be literally surrendering to the enemy, by admitting that state authority has been inappropriately directed at drug users.[33]

The 1992 edition of the *National Drug Control Strategy* is much less strident in tone, and clearly recognizes certain legal drugs—notably alcohol and nicotine—as part of the drug problem, but the legalistic-moralistic approach remains alive and well. User accountability retains its central position: "In short, the drug problem reflects bad decisions by people with free wills."[34] Moreover,

> Holding casual users accountable for their actions through criminal, civil, and social sanctions is intergral to the National Drug Control Strategy. . . . On the presumption that law enforcement not only punishes but also instructs, laws and policies directed toward holding users accountable deter drug use by providing clear consequences for possessing or using illegal drugs.[35]

The policy eschews any socio-economic influences on the choice to take up drugs (even though on the same page it invokes such influences as part of the effort to keep people away from drugs).[36]

The *National Drug Control Strategy* for 1992 seems to describe a major effort to legislate individual and public morality, and to do this over a rather short period of time as social changes go. This is in contrast to possible alternative efforts to encourage the more gradual emergence of a moral stand on drugs of all kinds through building a more humane—may I say "kinder and gentler?"—society. The *National Drug Control Strategy* seeks to press people—through cajolery, threat, punishment, and, yes, education and treatment—to be more like the moral center, like "us," the rule writers and law enforcers, like the second and third drug cultures.

Overall, the *National Drug Control Strategy* is a fascinating document. From the perspective of the drug warriors and the drug-fearing parts of the public for whom the elimination of (illegal) drugs is the absolute top national priority, it couldn't be better. The reach of the law into every nook and cranny of private and public life to search out and punish any kind of user and any level of dealer is exquisite and becoming more so each year: By October 1993, all states must mandate a six-month suspension of driver's licenses for people convicted of any drug offense (never mind that possessing a leaf of marijuana in one's attic bears no relation to driving skill) or face a 5 percent reduction in federal highway funds. States are urged to pass laws such that conviction of any drug offense could lead to suspension of licenses for barbers, physicians, beauticians, lawyers, and plumbers (among others); eviction from public housing units; and loss of state funded benefits, such as student loans. The list goes on and on. From the perspective of people concerned for the economic and social costs of the drug war and its effects on civil liberties, the *National Drug Control Strategy* is in all too many respects a document to be feared. In later chapters we will see more of the reasons why.

HOW OTHER COUNTRIES HANDLE THEIR DRUG PROBLEMS

Against the background of the bleak situation represented in our three drug cultures, it may be helpful to see if other countries' ways of dealing with their drug problems offer some ideas that might be useful in our own.

Most other nations have both drug abuse problems and laws and practices to cope with them; drug abuse is a multinational problem. It is also a problem between nations, an international problem, as well. This fact is represented in two important treaties developed by the World Health Organization (WHO), The Single Convention on Narcotic Drugs (1961) and the Convention on Psychotropic Drugs (1971). Most of the world's countries are signators of these conventions. The conventions obligate the contracting parties to take all practicable measures to prevent abuse of drugs, to provide early identification, treatment, and education of drug abusers; to promote the training of staff to provide treatment and after-care for drug abusers; to establish centers for research and education designed to cope with problems arising from the use of illegal drugs; and to provide training for other people involved with the country's drug problem.

The conventions do not specify in detail what each signator country must do, in recognition of the large differences in cultures, problems, and economic means among the countries. Even though the United States, with its much sterner anti-drug policies, has always been the prime mover behind international drug agreements, the treaties do generate incentives to develop policies that are more rather than less homogeneous in order to facilitate international controls on drug production and trafficking, including cooperation among law enforcement agencies of the signator countries.

The WHO has published a number of documents designed to clarify issues and provide guidance in pursuing the conventions' objectives. The United Nations, through its Division on Narcotic Drugs, has emphasized the seriousness of the problems connected with illicit drugs in several important documents, such as a legal guide on electronic fund transfers, and set of strategies and policies for drug control, among others. The resulting interconnectedness of drug policies of the more than one hundred countries that are parties to these conventions poses formidable obstacles to the advocacy of drug legalization in the United States as the solution to America's drug problem. In spite of the arguments that can be offered in favor of one or another form of legalization, no one country could easily just rear back and legalize drugs without provoking criticism and possible other consequences from other countries.

The drug problem is a world problem. To get a better understanding of this fact and to anticipate the difficulties in making major changes in U.S. policy, at least in the short run, it will be helpful to look more specifically at how a number of other countries face up to it. The summaries that follow derive from a 1989 report published by the Max Planck Institute for Foreign and International Penal Law, prepared in anticipation of the gradual fading away of national borders in Europe scheduled to begin in 1992.[37] (I have omitted The Netherlands from this review, for it is covered more extensively in Chapter 5.)

The most general thing that can be said about drug policies in Western Europe is that the standard drugs of abuse—marijuana, cocaine, heroin, and their derivatives, along with various psychotropic synthetics—have been, and remain, illegal. Within this framework, the most general thing to be said is that there are great differences among the countries in what they do about drugs. Subordinate to this generalization is that trafficking and dealing are much more avidly prosecuted and severely punished than consumption and the acts leading to consumption, and that there are vast differences in the ways that uses of "soft" drugs are treated. Finally, no European country is as fierce in its pursuit of traffickers, dealers, and especially users as is the United States. No European country has "declared war" on drugs.

Austria

Austrian drug law distinguishes clearly between user and dealer, with the idea of punishing dealers severely, and users as little as possible, preferring a resort to treatment and other efforts to get users to become non-users. Indeed, the largest responsibility under the law resides with the Ministry of Health, not with law enforcement agencies. The legislature is said to be in a dilemma, having to respond to public concerns over the illegality of trafficking and the hazards of use while following the general guidance of experts who expect little benefit from criminalizing drug use.

The result is that prohibitions against trafficking are made stiffer while user punishments decline, and treatment requirements increase. Possession of a minor quantity of a drug for personal use typically results in a two-year probationary period, depending on advice from health authorities. Abusers are looked on as sick and are offered a choice difficult to refuse: treatment or punishment. A person suspected of using or abusing (no distinction is made here) drugs may be reported to the Ministry of Health, which must determine the suspect's condition through an obligatory examination. If the suspect is determined to be drug-dependent and could profit from treatment, the health authority can order and monitor treatment. If the user is found to be not yet addicted, the authority can order treatment only with the individual's consent. Treatment facilities that are certified by the government receive subsidies for treatment costs.

The reality of the distinction between abuser and dealer is hard to maintain, however, for, as in every country, abusers often have to be dealers in order to afford their habits. Thus they run a double risk and, when caught, choose to appear as abusers if they can, hoping for a civil commitment instead of a criminal conviction. Even so, dealers who deal to support their personal habits are likely to receive more lenient punishment than vocational dealers.

Penalties for trafficking violations tend to be mild when compared with American standards. An importer, exporter, producer, or distributor of illicit drugs in major quantities may get a prison term of up to five years. A quantity is "major" if its transmittal would present an extensive public health hazard. Sentence length may also be extended if the convicted person is a member of a criminal drug distributing organization (up to ten years), has a previous conviction for a similar offense or deals in very large quantities (up to fifteen years).

How well does Austrian policy work? Drug use delinquency rose rather sharply from 1968 to 1974; continued to rise rather slowly from 1975, when 2,287 people were charged and 686 convicted; to 1981, when 5,804 were charged and 1803 were convicted. Since then the trend has been generally downward, with 4,739 being charged and 1,238 convicted in 1986.[38] This trend is reported to be continuing, with young people not being attracted to a hard-core drug ideology and tending to prefer cannabis and other soft drugs and to avoid heroin and cocaine.

Britain

American drug reform advocates in the 1960s used to point to Britain as having the right orientation to heroin—a "medico-centric" one in which maintenance doses and the substitute methadone were available on prescription from physicians and the costs of habit-supporting crime were down. Something went wrong, however, partly because of leakage from authorized recipients to others, partly because of the growth of heroin popularity among young working-class males, which resulted in a rapid rise in abuse and related costs in health and crime, and partly from the growing impatience of conservative governments.

With the passage of the Misuse of Drugs Bill in 1971, the United Kingdom abandoned the "addict as victim" concept and adopted a strong crime control perspective. The law abolished the distinction between narcotics and other drugs, prohibited physicians from prescribing certain suspectedly risky drugs, and divided drugs into three classes for purposes of punishment. Class A drugs included heroin, other opiates, cocaine, and LSD; conviction of possession of these can produce a maximum sentence of seven years. Being convicted of possessing Class B drugs, including cannabis, can bring a maximum of five years. Possessing Class C drugs, mainly amphetamines, can earn the offender two years in jail. As in other countries, promoting drug use is treated more harshly. Trafficking, producing, and possessing with intent to distribute Class A drugs can lead to a sentence of life in prison; with Class B and C drugs, the sentence can reach fourteen years. Consumption of opiates and ownership of opium pipes and other related utensils, or managing premises permitting the use of opiates can produce a sentence of fourteen years in prison. In this conversion to an American style criminalization approach to the drug problem, treatment and maintenance have continued, but are decidedly less prominent in British policy and practice.

Not surprisingly, the new orientation has led to a steady increase in the number of police specializing in drug investigation, and a corresponding decline in police resources directed into other areas, such as fraud. There has also been an increase of around 300 percent in the number of people incarcerated, from 711 in 1979 to 2825 in 1986. Sentence lengths have also increased, as has the use of custodial sentences compared with probationary sentences.[39] Students of the problem have yet to conclude if the beneficial effects on drug use and abuse outweigh the costs of an expanded criminal justice system and of attendant risks to civil liberties.

Sweden

In Sweden, the Narcotics Drug Act of 1968 as amended through 1985 covers all forms of drug handling and use. Production, possession with intent to distribute, actual distribution, packaging, storing, negotiating contracts between buyers and sellers, even possession for personal use, selling or supplying needles or syringes—all are criminal acts. No distinction is made between hard and soft drugs.

Relatively intense policing of drug problems is widely practiced. Every county has its special drug unit, and the number of police assigned purely to drug cases rose from 31 in 1965 to 523 in 1986.[40]

Penalties for minor offenses, such as possession for personal use, are relatively light, ranging from fines to a maximum of six months in jail. What are called simple offenses, such as possessing more than a day or two of supply and suggesting an intent to distribute, can draw a jail sentence of three years. Serious offenses, involving large quantities and clear plans or actions to distribute or to import drugs are punishable by maximum sentences of ten years. These are relatively few such offenses, however, amounting to only four percent of drug arrests in 1986; the most common offense is simple possession, which in 1986 accounted for 68 percent of offenses.[41] Addicts may be hospitalized for treatment without their consent when they appear to be endangering their health. However, treatment in general is not a prominent part of Swedish policy.

Italy

In contrast to the policies of Britain and Sweden, Italy's approach is much milder. Its 1975 law was among the first in Europe to introduce the general view of non-punishment for the user while retaining the threat of punishment for the pusher. Heroin, cocaine, cannabis, and synthetic psychotropics remain illegal, and any activities linked to drug pushing and possessing substantial quantities of drugs are punishable offenses. Yet the law allows penalty exceptions for buying and possessing drugs for personal use; needles and syringes are not outlawed. The habitual user is not considered a criminal but rather a person to be cured, rehabilitated, and returned to society. This is not to say that use of illegal drugs has broad permission or de facto legalization, for police can seize any amount of drugs and bring even a modest user to court. At the time of sentencing, the court may offer the choice to undergo treatment or serve time in prison.

Trafficking is subject to much stricter control and can lead to more serious consequences. Four to fifteen years in prison and a very substantial fine can follow conviction on charges of producing, offering, selling, transporting, importing, or exporting hard drugs. In the case of soft drugs, the prison term can be two to six years accompanied by a somewhat lesser fine. If quantitites are small, but still in excess of what is normally considered for personal use, lesser prison terms may be assigned.

As in other European countries, there is discussion of the prospect of fully legalizing some of the now proscribed drugs. However, there appears to be a trend in Italian drug law toward further depenalizing and liberalizing the consumption of soft drugs, a trend that has undercut demands for outright legalization.

CONCLUSION

The group of scholars and professionals convened by the Max Planck Institute to review and analyze drug policies in Western Europe tend to agree that the repression-criminalization orientation to drugs produces many of the same problems we see in the United States—high costs, risks to civil liberties, corruption of police, needless marginalizing of people for minor user offenses—and offers little hope of producing anything approximating a society free of drugs. Even the chief law enforcement officer in the city of Utrecht, The Netherlands, asserts that the repressive strategy has failed, and calls for policies that would emphasize other goals, such as integrating drugs into social life as we try to do with alcohol and nicotine, educating people about drugs, and managing abuse rather than trying to stamp it out via the criminal justice system.[42] These scholars also see little hope of major reform in drug policies toward greater liberalization in view of the widespread fear of drugs that has taken root in all of their countries.

SOME TRAPS

Before leaving this introductory chapter I want to present a view held by a small but growing number of scholars of the drug problem, a view with which I am in agreement. A major part of the problem is a combination of semantics and the American culture. It is part of our tradition to reify problems, to think of them as "things" to be attacked, warred upon, expunged, exterminated, or otherwise gotten rid of. We do not think of problems as processes to be understood and gradually transformed; that is altogether too complicated and unthrilling. Fighting wars, real wars against real and threatening countries, mobilizes energy in ways that mere solving of problems simply cannot, for the simple reason that such wars indeed threaten our persons, families, and institutions. Calling a program designed to relieve poverty or a particular illness a "war" is essentially a propagandistic device to justify whatever the program leaders think should be done. Before long the complexity of the problem and the futility of some of the actions taken in the name of removing "it" become apparent—

but the call to war is repeatedly sounded: "Give us the tools and we will finish the job!" (with deep apologies to Winston Churchill). The "war" and its rhetoric become institutionalized, and its slogans are believed and become common language: "Just say No!" What political leader wants to lose a war? Having declared the drug problem a national menace worthy of having a war declared on it traps us all into supporting the endless battles and all those brave things that warriors are supposed to do. Thus the war seems to take on a life of its own and becomes the powerful second drug culture, struggling to win the unwinnable and demanding ever more commitment from the third drug culture for the money, manpower, and legislation that must follow.

On a less grand scale, the tendency to think of problems as things confuses the way we think about drugs. In the rhetoric of committed drug warriors, drugs are in themselves bad. "They" do bad things to people. "They" get hold of us and make us powerless slaves to "them." "The trouble with drugs is not that they are illegal but that they destroy people. . . . And they destroy neighborhoods, communities—who knows, perhaps whole cities may go down," says Midge Decter.[43]

Also, we too often think of the over-use of drugs as a "disease" to be stamped out, as though by some superb treatment. This view runs the risk of turning over to the medical profession the responsibility and authority to try to straighten out a social problem whose complexity is far beyond the competence of any one profession. It is more reasonable, I think, to conceive the over-use of drugs as the result of a choice that the users have made and which they can be helped to unmake if they wish to do so. Aside from suggesting an avenue into a complex process that the disease concept tends to preclude, thinking of drug use—or abuse, or addiction—as a behavior pattern entered into as a conscious choice confers more dignity on the abuser or addict than labelling her as a "victim" for whom someone else has the responsibility to help or protect. More of this later.

So let this chapter conclude with the assertion that began it. The United States does have a serious set of problems—political, economic, medical, ethical, cultural, conceptual—connected with the production, sale, and use of illegal drugs. In the next chapter, we take up in more detail an analysis of the many kinds of costs that the drug problem imposes on our society and on other countries. An understanding of these costs will lead to a consideration of alternative policies and action programs that could make a positive difference in the way we might cope with—possibly even reduce—the problem.

Chapter 2

Documenting the Costs of the Drug Problem

All government policies have costs, even policies that do not have action programs attached to them. The laissez-faire policies with regard to industrial expansion and the use of children and unorganized adults in the work force during the late nineteenth and early twentieth centuries had heavy costs in poor child health and restricted life expectancies. The mix of today's policies about the use of illicit drugs also has costs as well as benefits.

In this chapter, I will summarize the major costs that we can attribute to the nation's problems with illicit drugs. Before getting into the facts of the matter, however, I want to make it clear that the prospect of reducing the economic costs of the drug problem will not alone persuade advocates of the drug war to back off from their enthusiasm. The motivations underlying both the drug-use problem and the drug-war problem are more complex than can be revealed through simple economic trade-offs. Wars are typically pursued because of conviction in the righteousness of a cause and fears of a perceived enemy and are sustained by beliefs that the values to be preserved can in no way be expressed in the language of economic costs and benefits. Nonetheless, I assert that the current war on drugs is indeed more a metaphor—a bogeyman that has emerged from the efforts to control illicit drugs and from the fears that sustain them—than a real nation-threatening, international conflict, regardless of how the most dedicated drug warriors see it. Therefore, as we build the case for a different way of dealing with the drug problem, I believe that it will be useful to portray in some detail the many kinds of costs that Americans continue to inflict on themselves and others through the drug war.

Most of these costs are associated with action programs that have been established in order to ameliorate various problems connected with drug use. It is the task of policy makers to seek out policies and to define their objectives so as to maximize the balance of public goods over the public afflictions wrought by the problem that policy makers are charged to reduce. Though economics underlies and guides most of our thinking on public issues—like making our industries more efficient and more competitive with those of other countries or restoring a more healthful air quality or improving national defense—economic values are insufficient. I believe that money and its uses mediate most aspects of national aspirations, be they housing, security, health, education, recreation, or any of many other aspects of human development. Money doesn't define the goals, however, it only tells us something—not everything—about how we arrange them in our hierarchy of values.

ECONOMIC COSTS

Turning now to the topic of costs, the first part of the chapter deals mainly with money in one form or another and how it is involved in the drug problem: money spent directly to prevent drug use; money spent to relieve the pain of drug use; money spent to understand the causes and treatment of drug use; money spent to discover, prosecute, and punish people who break drug laws; and even invisible money—money not collected in taxes on the sale of drugs. Having an understanding of these money costs can give us a good idea of how the drug problem and what we are doing about it stands in our hierarchy of fears and goals. Later in the chapter, I raise issues about values that are not easily translated into money language—the "non-monetizeable" costs of broken homes, uneducated teen-agers, fear-ridden neighborhoods, badly over-crowded court agendas—and show how some of these situations are impacted by the drug problem.

Trying to "cost out" the national drug problem is a formidable task, to say the least, one loaded with opportunities for procedural error, confused by the non-quantifiability of many important costs, beset by risks of miscellaneous misunderstandings, and fraught with basic philosophical disagreement on such topics as individual freedom, basic civil liberties, and the role of government in managing the private lives of citizens. But to make progress toward eventually relieving the country of the major afflictions of drug use and the scourge of the drug war, it is absolutely necessary to make the effort. Then it may be possible to discern some areas in which costs can be reduced and the general welfare enhanced.

In addition to the two general classes of internal costs just described, there is a sub-class of hard-to-define costs that lies outside our borders: the effects of our drug problem and the associated efforts to cope with it that fall on the people and institutions of countries that are engaged in satisfying U.S. appetites for illicit drugs. And these costs are not limited to the particular countries that are involved—Colombia, Bolivia, and Peru, to name only three examples—but, as we shall see, redound adversely on American interests.

Turning first to the domestic economic costs of the drug problem, a recently published study by Dorothy Rice[1] and her colleagues at the University of California at San Francisco, reported under the title *Economic Costs of Alcohol, Drug Abuse, and Mental Illness*, reveals much, but assuredly not all, about the dollar costs of the drug problem.

Before getting into numbers, I should note that the very breadth and complexity of the drug problem makes it impossible to produce a unified summary of its costs at any particular time. The Rice study was nearly five years in the making and gives us a good picture of the economic costs as of 1985, with estimates brought up to 1988 by extrapolating some major trends. Other cost estimates have been made by numerous analysts at different times. All produced big numbers. I lean on the Rice study because its categorical breakdowns are especially helpful in developing policy alternatives.

The analysis by Rice and her colleagues reveals a total 1985 cost of $44.052 billion. This number comes from two major categories of costs, "core costs" and "other related costs," both of which are interesting and have important implications for national drug policy. Table 2.1 summarizes them and includes, for comparison, Rice's cost calculations for the alcohol abuse problem, to which we will return in Chapter 5.

"Core costs" are simply the sum of the direct costs of treatment and the support of treatment through research and staff training—in hospitals, clinics, physicians' offices, and specialized treatment communities—plus the indirect costs of drug users being non-productive while sick or dead earlier than expected. These core costs come to about $10.624 billion.

"Other related costs" shown in detail in Table 2.2 are the most interesting from the standpoint of altering policy and will be discussed at greater length in Chapter 5. For the present, let it be noted that the approximately $22 billion total by which these costs for the drug problem exceed their counterparts for the alcohol problem is due largely to the "war on drugs,"

Table 2.1

Economic Costs of Alcohol and Drug Use
by Type of Cost, 1985
(from Rice et al., 1990)*

Type of Cost	Amount ($ millions)	
	Alcohol	Drugs
TOTAL	70,388	44,052
Core Costs	58,151	10,624
Direct	6;810	2,082
Treatment	6,315	1,881
Support	495	201
Indirect	51,371	8,542
Morbidity	27,388	5,979
Mortality	23,983	2,563
Other Related Costs	10,546	32,461
Direct	7,830	13,209
Indirect	3,166	19,252
Special Disease Groups	1,611	967
AIDS	–	967
Fetal alcohol syndrome	1,611	–

* The entries in this table and in Table 2.2 are gross summaries of detailed analyses of several sources developed in the Rice study. In the report, they are backed up by additional tables that show the cost components underlying each of the entries shown here. The report also states in detail the methodologies used to determine estimates of cost elements that may be unclear or ambiguous.

Table 2.2

Other Related Direct and Indirect Costs of Alcohol and Drug Use, 1985
(Rice et al., 1990)

Type of Cost	Amount ($ millions)	
	Alcohol	Drugs
TOTAL	10,546	32,461
Direct Costs	7,380	13,209
Crime	4,251	13,203
Public Expenditures	3,734	11,063
Criminal justice system	3,734	9,508
Police protection	1,338	5,810
Legal and adjudicative	274	1,108
State & federal corrections	884	2,130
Local corrections	1,238	460
Drug traffic control	–	1,555
Prevention	–	175
Law enforcement	–	1,380
Private legal defense	342	1,381
Property destruction	175	759
Other direct expenditures	3,129	6
Motor vehicle crashes	2,584	–
Fire destruction	457	–
Social welfare administration	88	6
Indirect Costs	3,166	19,252
Victims of crime	465	842
Incarceration	2,701	4,434
Crime careers	–	13,976

not to the use of drugs. These "other related costs" come to $32.461 billion, and they, too, have "direct" and "indirect" categories. The largest set of direct costs comes from $13.209 billion worth of crime. This figure in turn is made up of the following: $11.063 billion in public expenditures for the criminal justice system (police protection, criminal courts, probation and parole supervisors, prisons), $1.381 billion for private legal defense, and $759 million in property damage. Against figures like these, one is tempted to ignore an additional $6 million in social welfare administration, principally for vocational counseling.

The "indirect" portion of "other related costs" of $19.252 billion comes from $842 million in losses to victims of crime, from incarcerated law violators being non-productive to the tune of $4.434 billion, and from crime careers costing the public $13.976 billion in time that could otherwise have been productively used. This figure, incidentally, includes the losses in productivity arising from the several hundred young people killed annually in turf battles—most of violent urban "street crime"—over who is going to sell illicit drugs where. The President's Commission on Organized Crime estimates about 70 drug-market murders occur each year in Miami alone.[2] If the estimated overall increase of 25% in costs from the 1985 data base that Rice et al. used is added in, the figure is another $14.2 billion, for a total of $58.3 billion in 1988—an amount that begins to look significant even if compared to defense budgets. One must wonder what good might otherwise be done with some of this money.

These figures do not yet represent all of the dollar costs. President Bush's proposed 1993 budget includes several categories of money that do not appear in Rice's calculations for 1985 or in the 1988 update. Requests for the national drug control strategy are summarized in Table 2.3; their total of $6.107 billion exceeds Rice's 1985 estimates of $1.555 billion for law enforcement by 392 percent. The entries in the table are not directly comparable to the breakdown of Rice's entry shown in Table 2.2, so I cannot conclude that all of the Table 2.3 entries are clear categorical additions to Rice's totals; nonetheless, they merit comment.

Especially notable is the cost of interdicting drugs that various people are trying to ship into the United States from other places; this cost involves the Coast Guard, the Department of Defense, the Immigration and Naturalization Service, and the Customs Service, which would spend another $2.2 billion. The foreign aid component of $768 million is to be used, among other purposes, to induce other countries, such as Bolivia and Peru, to cut down on one of their major sources of foreign exchange—the growing and

Table 2.3

Federal Budget Request for Drug Law Enforcement, fiscal year 1993 ($ millions)

Organized Crime and Drug Enforcement Task Forces (OCDETF)	399
Drug Enforcement Administration (DEA)	788
Federal Bureau of Investigation (FBI)	206[b]
U. S. Attorneys and U. S. Marshals [a]	235
Internal Revenue Service [a]	111
Federal Bureau of Prisons	1,400[b]
International anti-drug programs	768
Interdiction	2,200
TOTAL	6,107

[a] Not represented in calculations of Rice et al.

[b] From fiscal year 1992 budget; not broken out specifically in 1993 request.

selling of coca—and to allow U.S. military forces to come into their countries to help them do that. In addition, the FBI would come in for $206 million, the Organized Crime Drug Enforcement Task Forces for $399 million, and the Drug Enforcement Administration for $788 million; here there is much additional money being spent on trying to enforce the anti-drug laws. Finally, another $1.4 billion can be added for the Federal Bureau of Prisons, which would need another 2450 new cells in which to house and feed prisoners. About $540 million of this would be a "one-time" cost of constructing the new prisons. (Figures for the FBI and Bureau of Prisons are estimates based on the 1992 proposed budget. Their drug war components were not broken out in the 1993 proposed budget.)

It is tempting to imagine another cost in the form of taxes lost to local, state, and federal governments by not being collected on an estimated $14 billion worth of street-level sales of marijuana.[3] A possible total tax take of, say, 40 percent, or about $5.6 billion, could go a long way toward funding a lot of worthwhile activities, or even saving taxpayers some money. Such an estimate, however, would overstate the possible return from the only market in which such taxes could be collected—a legalized one—for in such a market, the price of marijuana would be dramatically lower than at present.

Wars are expensive, even if they exist only in myriad scattered episodes of drug busts, arrests, prosecutions, incarcerations, parole supervisions, publicity and rhetoric, rather than on traditional battlefields. This one, including treatment, prevention, and research, seems to be costing at least $60 billion each year but is surely more than this, given the age of some of our cost figures. If this amount of money suggests that something better might be done with much of it than to have it consumed or lost in various ways as a result of trying to contain the drug problem, you are on the brink of discovering new options for a national drug policy. We'll take up this topic in Chapters 5 and 6.

NON-MONETIZEABLE COSTS

Costs that cannot be measured in dollar terms are the most difficult to deal with when thinking about public policy. What costs occur when a family breaks up or when a teenager is killed in a street fight or when a neighborhood is deemed unsafe by many of its families or when people are afraid to say No if a police offcer asks to see what is in a paper bag, or when a dispute between landlord and tenant cannot be processed in a court because the court is loaded with hundreds of cases of drug possession charges? Few will deny that real costs are connected with such situations, or that they are hard to figure out. The field of welfare economics has long addressed these cost problems, and efforts to assign dollar values to them have been made. Surely a family break-up costs money in legal fees, additional housing and other living costs, but the future costs—possibly of welfare payments, health care costs, police and court expenses that are borne by the community—are much harder to estimate.

Does the early death of a teen ager cost society something beyond funeral expenses? One can argue that it depends on who the teen ager was—a potential thief and murderer or an engineering genius—and make some guess about the possible loss to society due to this "premature" death. Domestic airlines some years ago ordinarily assigned an average value of $250,000 in calculating funds needed to settle death claims after fatal crashes. Today, according to the Air Transport Association, no standard figure enters into the airlines' negotiations of premiums for the standard $100 million per incident of liability coverage. The actual monetary value of lost lives is left to the settlement process between airlines and crash victims' estates. The average settlement remains close to $250,000.[4] No one has yet produced a workable answer to the question: How valuable is a human life, independent of that person's potential role in society? Surely no dollar answer can be assigned, but the value is not thereby eliminated.

The same goes for individual civil liberties, which are protected by the Bill of Rights, the first ten amendments to the Constitution. We spend countless dollars and hours defending against infringements of these rights in courts across the country—freedom of speech, freedom from unreasonable search and seizure are values we hold dear, but no one seriously tries to hang a dollar sign on them.

Thus, when dealing with these hard-to-cost aspects of life—such as police, court, and incarceration costs arising from crime in deteriorating neighborhoods— we have to do the best we can to estimate their value but then proceed on the beliefs that, Yes, having neighborhoods with poor housing and disordered schools is bad; that, Yes, it is bad, not good, that young people get killed for whatever reason; that, Yes, a neighborhood where people are afraid to be on the streets ought to be free from crime; that, No, people should not be subjected to random searches and other invasions of privacy; and, that Yes, courts should be able to dispense justice expeditiously. It is in these areas where non-monetizeable values predominate that political beliefs and philosophies, rather than comparatively straightforward economic calculations, must prevail in the process of selecting and enforcing policies thought to be in the public interest. Here we turn more directly to look at these costs and how they are related to the drug problem.

Deterioration of Neighborhoods

The numbers of drug dealers, users, drug-related crimes, and arrests are clearly highest in overcrowded urban neighborhoods occupied by minorities and low-income families, characterized by poor housing and lax public services. Regrettably, from the standpoint of the analyst, it is virtually impossible to separate cause from effect: do already poor neighborhoods attract the drug trade, or does the drug trade ruin the neighborhoods? The statistical relationship is clear, but the causal connection is not. It is safe to say, however, that the two conditions feed on one another: drug dealers stand to make money selling drugs to people who are depressed, hopeless, angry with the world, or already addicted. Muggings and burglaries help to provide the cash with which to start or sustain a habit.

Probably the surest causal relationship is the one between the presence of drugs in a strong market and the number of dealers and occasional bystanders who are killed in wars between dealer groups over territories within the market area. Dealer-related violence may also extend to non-dealers who may witness violence, as in a New York case in which a witness was murdered apparently by defendants who were part of a drug-dealing gang. In another incident, a Brooklyn housewife was murdered in retaliation for her community activism against drug dealers.[5] A side effect of these wars is reported as an increase in the number of children needing counseling after witnessing or experiencing drug-related violence.[6] Another effect is the perpetuation of dealer as a vocation because of the higher income that dealers enjoy over ordinary street robbers and other people of similar ability who are employed in legitimate jobs.

Regardless of inability to tease out clear cause/effect relationships in the deterioration of drug-infested neighborhoods, no one can disagree that the elimination of drugs and dealers would be followed by improvements in neighborhoods. Just how this might be brought about will be the topic of later chapters.

Corruption

Corruption of police, prosecutors, parole officers, and other public officials is virtually concomitant with the trade in illegal drugs. A well-functioning black market simply demands the illicit services of law enforcement agents of all types. These people command, and often have for sale, a very valuable service: the non-enforcement of the law. And the sellers of this service suffer no threat from customers dissatisfied with high prices: the trafficker required to ante up a payoff to a policeman or a Customs Service inspector is in no position to complain, and must accept making pay-offs as a part of the cost of doing business, which is recovered through the prices paid by customers. Steven Wisotsky's summary of the corruption problem cites a report that New York City street dealers in heroin paid as much as 40 percent of gross sales in bribes to avoid arrest.[7] The actual cost of corruption is extremely hard to calculate, beyond the mere counting of corruption arrests and indictments, but it shows up in the growth of cynicism on the part of law enforcement people as they see dealers plying their trade in the presence of officers looking the other way, or as they read of arrested dealers getting off with purchased light sentences or probationary periods.

Overload of the Courts

With increasing drug-related cases and the resulting deferral in handling other seemingly less urgent court business, another cost of the drug problem is created. In 1985 there were more than 800,000 arrests for various drug law violations. John Martin has documented the effects of this through an analysis of court case loads in a number of cities, as shown in Table 2.4.[8]

What this means is that cases involving divorce, property damage claims, child abuse, libel, embezzlement, and the rest of the everyday run of criminal and civil offenses must wait in a long line of politically popular drug cases, most of which involve offenses that are consensual (dealing) or victimless (possession).

In addition to the "mere" inconvenience of having civil and other non-drug cases deferred, this condition represents an infringement of Sixth Amendment rights to a speedy trial by jury in criminal cases because of the long delays that are developing. The situation is made worse partly because prosecuting attorneys are being hired at a rate faster than judgeships are being created to handle the cases.

The Assault on Civil Liberties

Here we have an increasingly dangerous cost stemming from the nation's drug problem. The Fourth Amendment reads:

Table 2.4

Percent of Drug Related Cases in Selected Municipal Courts
(Martin, 1990)

COURT	%1983	%1987	% change
Boston	16	44	+175
Jersey City	21	45	+114
Bronx	22	46	+107
Oakland	19	37	+95
Pittsburgh	7	13	+86
Portland	10	18	+80
Miami	19	33	+74
New Orleans	20	32	+60
San Diego	18	28	+56
Providence	20	30	+50
Wichita	12	17	+42
Cleveland	12	17	+42
Minneapolis	19	10	+11
Dayton	11	12	+9
Newark	40	42	+5
Phoenix	23	24	+4
Detroit	20	20	+0
AVERAGE	17.6	27.5	+56.2

The right of the people to be secure in their persons, houses, papers, and effects, against unreasonable search and seizure, shall not be violated, and no warrants shall issue, but upon probable cause, supported by oath or affirmation, and particularly describing the place to be searched, and the persons or things to be seized.

So wrote the framers of the Constitution, intending to protect the citizens against intrusions from a strong federal government. After the Fourteenth Amendment was ratified in 1868, several Supreme Court cases extended to citizens the same protection against intrusions by the states. In 1928 Justice Louis Brandeis wrote what became for many years the established interpretation of the Fourth Amendment:[9]

The makers of our Constitution undertook to secure conditions favorable to the pursuit of happiness. They recognized the significance of man's spiritual nature, of his feeling, and of his intellect. They knew that only a part of the pain, pleasure, and satisfactions of life are to be found in material things. They sought to protect Americans in their beliefs, their thoughts, their emotions, and their sensations. They conferred, as against the government, the right to be let alone—the most comprehensive of rights and the right most valued by civilized men. To protect that right, every unjustifiable intrusion by the Government upon the privacy of the individual, whatever the means employed, must be deemed a violation of the Fourth Amendment.

The drug problem and the attendant wars on it have set these grand phrases aside, with appellate court concurrences in the requirement that suspected drug users may be subjected to urine tests, school locker searches made without probable cause, and rectal examination made of incoming travelers if customs agents suspect they might be carrying drugs internally.[10] Unlike most crimes against persons or property, drug dealing crimes are usually carried out between two or more willing people, and thus there is no complaint to initiate police action. But in the pursuit of offenders in the drug wars, drug agents must intrude into the private lives of suspected, not accused, citizens, producing another drug problem cost.

Lest the literature on Fourth Amendment incursions convey the impression that poor and powerless people are the main victims, we should note that involuntary drug testing is spreading rapidly into the middle class. A summary article in the *New York Times* reports that 75 percent of 1200 companies responding in 1992 to a questionnaire from the American Management Association test for controlled and illegal substances (not alcohol, that is), a rate that is 18 percent greater than in the preceding year.[11] This is an outgrowth of the Drug-Free Workplace Act of 1988, which requires companies with U.S. government contracts to have drug policies and make efforts to have work places free of drugs, whether or not there is solid evidence that ordinary drug users perform less well at work or have higher accident rates. Companies are increasingly willing, it seems, to trade off privacy against what they believe to be work place risks.

The "exclusionary rule," established in the 1914 case of Weeks *v.* United States[12] as a means of enforcing the Fourth Amendment, prevents in federal courts the use against suspected offenders of accidentally obtained evidence or evidence obtained in seeming violation of Fourth Amendment rights. The rule was extended to apply to the state courts and state law enforcement officers in 1961, through the case of Mapp *v.* Ohio.[13] In recent years the rule has been steadily eroded in Supreme Court decisions that have invented a number of exceptions, such as the claimed exercise of "good faith" in making arrests at mistaken addresses that happen to produce evidence of an offense not under investigation.[14]

Eric Sterling, President of the Criminal Justice Policy Foundation and for ten years counsel to the House Judiciary Committee, provides us with a chilling summary of how the Bill of Rights is becoming a casualty in the drug war,[15] as is clear from the following few examples:

First Amendment and the free exercise of religion was involved in the case of two Native Americans discharged from employment in an Oregon drug treatment program because they used peyote as part of the religious practices of the Native American Church. Applying for unemployment benefits, they were denied them, and the two sued. The Oregon Supreme Court found that they were entitled to benefits because they were using peyote as a function of their religious practices. The Oregon Attorney General, however, arguing that a drug treatment program requires a drug-free staff, carried the case to the U.S. Supreme Court, which reversed the Oregon Court. This may seem a trivial case in the grand scheme of constitutional law, but note: (1) the two Native Americans were never charged with a law violation; (2) peyote is used by more than 250,000 Native American worshipers who consider peyote no more a drug than Christians do wine in communion rites; (3) there is no evidence of anyone being harmed by the religious use of peyote; (4) twenty-three states and the federal government exempt the religious use of peyote from the Controlled Substances Act. In his dissent, Justice Harry Blackmun wrote, "One hopes that the Court is aware of the consequences, and that its result is not a product of overreaction to the serious problems the country's drug crisis has generated."

The *Fourth Amendment* protections against unreasonable searches and seizures have been watered down by legislated exceptions to warrant requirements and probable cause requirements. Sterling cites a story in *USA Today* of a Detroit police raid on a food market in a high drug-use neighborhood. After their dog sniffed cocaine on three one dollar bills in the cash register, the police held the store owner and seized his profits. This prompted a federal district judge to "wonder where the United States is headed. My concern is that the real victim of the war on drugs might be the constitutional rights of the American people."

A more frightening incident occurred in New Hampshire when police, armed with a search warrant based in part on an informant's tip that was nearly two years old, and with no evidence that the resident was armed, used a battering ram to enter his home at 5:00 A.M. on August 3, 1989. "As he rose from his bed, apparently resisting the intruders, Mr. Lavoie was fatally shot as his son watched. A single marijuana cigarette was found."

The *Eighth Amendment* protections against cruel and unusual punishment have been upheld by the Supreme Court's rejection of the death penalty in crimes that do not involve an intent to kill. On June 28, 1990, however, by a vote of 66 to 32, the Senate accepted an amendment to a bill that would permit the death penalty for a person convicted of a drug violation committed as part of a large-scale continuous criminal enterprise, regardless of whether or not a homicide had been committed. Though the amendment has not yet become law, its portent for legislative attitudes is unnerving.

COSTS IMPOSED ON OTHER COUNTRIES

There is still another set of costs that cannot be reckoned in dollars. These are the effects that have been wrought on other countries by the American appetite for drugs and by our wars on drugs.

American politicians and policy makers do not usually get worked up over the effects of U.S. actions on other normally friendly countries, since citizens of those countries do not vote in our elections. Nonetheless, the American effort over the past two decades to reduce the supply of illicit drugs heading our way has had nearly devastating repercussions in a number of countries whose cooperation in our drug wars we have sought. We have unwittingly encouraged the corruption of police forces, military forces, and justice departments.

In Colombia especially the war on drugs is leading to a serious risk that democratic institutions and processes could fail and be transformed to an autocratic structure, an outcome surely not desired by any U.S. administration. Corrupting effects in Mexico and other countries are also widely evident, as has been documented in a large and growing literature.[16] To make this point, let us look at some of the facts in Colombia particularly.

Probably more than any other country Colombia has borne the external costs of the U.S.'s drug problem, while a small number of processors and exporters of cocaine have grown rich beyond their fellow citizens' imaginations. Over the past twenty years or so, Colombia has emerged as the pre-eminent drug-trafficking country. Marijuana production boomed in the late '60s in response to growing U.S. demand, partly aided by Mexico's stricter enforcement of anti-drug laws. By the middle of the '70s, Colombia produced about 70 percent of the marijuana reaching the United States. Nearly 50,000 small farmers along the Colombian coastline depended on the marijuana crop for a living, with probably an equal number of dealers, bankers, transporters, guards and the like making significant portions of their living servicing the trade.

Cocaine became a significant commodity in the illicit drug market during the '70s, building on a centuries-old tradition of coca plant use by indigenous Indian groups who found that chewing the leaves not only gave them pleasure but made it possible to sustain hard work under difficult conditions. U.S. customs agents seized around 100 kilograms of Colombian cocaine in 1970, but thanks to the energetic entrepreneurship of Carlos Lehder Rivas and Jorge Luis Ochoa, notable among others, the coca industry grew rapidly. By 1976, an estimated 19 metric tons of cocaine entered the U.S. from Colombia, with the figure growing to an estimated 45 metric tons by 1991.[17] Revenues of this illegal trade are estimated at about $3 billion in 1988, a relatively small amount when compared to U.S. budgets (and deficits), but bringing with it enormous economic power in a country whose gross domestic product from legitimate enterprises came to about $35.4 billion.[18] Traffickers based in the city of Medellín began reaching for political power, buying interest in radio stations and newspapers, and cultivating political followings in cities by building low-income housing and handing out cash.

Until the 1970s, Colombian governments did little to interfere in trafficking, though it was obliged as a signator country to the Single Convention of 1961 to criminalize trafficking in marijuana, cocaine, and heroin. In 1977, yielding to continuing U.S. persuasion, President Afredo Lopez Michelsen expanded the campaign against cocaine traffic, backed by assistance from the Carter administration. President Julio Cesar Turbay Ayala, three months after taking office in 1978, used his state-of-seige powers to crack down on drug traffickers. The U.S. government proposed, and President Turbay agreed to, a treaty that would permit Colombian traffickers accused of crimes in the U.S. to be extradited and tried in U.S. courts. The U.S. tripled its foreign aid to Colombia.

This combination of the extradition treaty and the foreign aid incentive to help in the U.S. drug war created the conditions for extensive corruption of the Colombian police and courts. The huge amounts of money available to the traffickers were used effectively to buy information from police about potential drug raids, and to buy from judges dismissals of charges or light sentences for convicted traffickers. In a despairing comment, President Turbay noted that "Colombians are not corrupting Americans. You are corrupting us. If you abandon illegal drugs, the traffic will disappear."[19] On the other side of the Colombian drug war, the same relationship is expressed by a leading trafficker, Gilberto Rodriguez Orejuela: "Economics has a natural law: Supply is determined by demand. When cocaine stops being consumed, when there's no demand for it . . . that will be the end of that business."[20]

In 1982, the new Colombian president, Belisario Betancur Cuartas, renounced the extradition treaty of 1979, preferring to try Colombian traffickers in Colombian courts. To placate expressions of outrage from Washington, Betancur appointed Rodriga Lara Bonilla to head the Justice Ministry and press more aggressively the drug war in cooperation with U.S. narcotics agents. After some initial successes by Lara's staff, the Medellín drug cartel put out a contract on Lara's life. It was carried out on April 30, 1984. Responding to public outrage, President Betancur signed an extradition order for Carlos Lehder Rivas and reinstated the treaty with the United States.

Betancur's extended war on drugs, urged and aided by the Americans, was met with skilled and fearsome response by the drug traffickers: they fought extradition by threatening and physically attacking the Colombian judiciary. Between 1981 and 1986, more than fifty judges, including a dozen members of the Supreme Court, were murdered. For example, on July 23, 1985, Superior Court Judge Tulio Manuel Castro Gil, who had charged that Pablo Escobar had planned the 1984 assassination of Justice Minister Lara Bonilla, was himself assassinated in Bogotá. And to demonstrate their reach, drug bosses arranged the near-fatal shooting of Enrico Parejo Gonzalez, President Betancur's second minister of justice, in Budapest, Hungary, where he had been sent as ambassador in an effort to spare his life.

Careers in the Colombian justice system were becoming increasingly hazardous. A 1991 newspaper account reports that to protect judges from reprisals administered by accused traffickers or their friends, Colombian courts have adopted the practice of screening judges from the view of the accused and using voice scramblers to further prevent their being identified.[21]

Other examples may be cited of the damage done to Colombian institutions of law enforcement and justice as a result of efforts to comply with U.S. demands for controlling the supply of drugs from that country. Bruce Bagley, political science professor at the University of Miami, has argued, "The Colombian government has been drafted to man the front lines of the drug war . . . with results that have been fatal for many Colombian officials and debilitating for the country's political system," while the U.S. government continues to insist that the Colombians continue to take on the drug lords no matter what the cost.[22] Increasing pressure from the U.S.—for example, by instituting lengthy customs checks for travelers and commercial goods arriving from Colombia and by threatening to de-certify Colombia as a country doing all it could against drug lords (thus to quality for U.S. aid)—has aroused Colombian nationalism and anti-U.S. resentment. Many Colombian and American students of the international drug scene are becoming concerned for the stability of democracy in Colombia.

Elaine Shannon, reporter and longtime analyst of the international drug traffic, poignantly describes the Colombian government's travails of being caught between the traffickers it cannot control and the American government it cannot please. *Desperados—Latin Drug Lords, U.S. Lawmen, and the War America Can't Win* is her book-length account of the impossible tasks demanded of U.S. and Latin American drug enforcement officers. In a chapter appropriately titled "Why Are We Bleeding Alone?" she relates the feelings of Colombian narcotics bureau chief Francisco Bernal: "We're being left to fight this war alone. We're supplying the dead, the country is being de-stabilized, and what are we getting?"[23] And Alfredo Gutierrez Marquez, Colombia's attorney general, suggested in 1988 that Colombia might have to legalize drugs and negotiate with the cartels. "We've had a row of corpses in Colombia, and yet the cocaine laboratories are still working, and the Medellín cartel members are free. . . . It's time we stopped playing the fool."[24]

Waves of violence have undermined citizen confidence in the Colombian government. Hard-liners call for increasing the involvement of the military in the war against drug lords, even at the cost of restrictions on democracy and civil liberties and rights. As Bagley writes, "In the final analysis, it is Colombia's democratic traditions and institutions that are at stake. The next U.S. administration must take care not to force Colombia into the abyss of authoritarianism in the name of national security and the war on drugs."[25]

Colombia is but one country paying the price of cooperation with the U.S. drug wars. President Paz Estensero of Bolivia was persuaded in 1986 by the threat of reduced U.S. foreign aid to "invite" American troops into his country to help close down cocaine refining sites. The effort was very unpopular among agricultural workers and their unions, thousands of whose jobs were threatened. All told, the operation was only partially successful, with new cocaine processing sites popping up in other locations as targeted sites were shut down. This action proved offensive to Bolivian nationalist pride and damaging to the already slender hard currency income from the cocaine trade, which not so incidentally, in 1986 was estimated to exceed by $200 million the sum of all legal exports.[26] The U.S. foreign aid reward fell far short of the hard currency loss, and the program was abandoned not long after it had begun.

Other book-length examinations of the impact of our drug war on Latin American countries reveal the same pattern of corruption and damage to institutions that we have seen in Colombia, though lacking in the widespread violence that Colombia has experienced. Peter Scott and Jonathan Marshall review the corrupting effects on the armies and law enforcement agencies in Central American countries in their book *Cocaine Politics: Drugs, Armies, and the CIA in Central America.* Shannon's *Desperados* recounts the Mexican experience in detail, using the assassination in Guadalajara of U.S. Drug Enforcement agent Enrique Camarena as the focal point of our difficult relations with Mexico in prosecuting the war on drugs.

A series of articles by Ethan Nadelmann has extensively documented the uniformly negative effects that the U.S. drug war has had on countries in Latin America and other parts of the world, and on other aspects of U.S. foreign policy as well.[27]

To deny that these are real costs of the American drug problem simply because they impact other countries is at best hypocritical. We should be concerned for the economic and political stability of those countries on humanitarian grounds alone, not to mention the importance of having healthy economies with which to trade, and stable governments with which to negotiate. And closer to the American politician's heart come the American taxpayer costs of these efforts, all of which have proven only partially effective—some would say utterly ineffective—as well as costly in actual dollar terms.

MORAL ISSUES

We will see more of the issue of drug policy morality in Chapter 6. The particular point to be made here is that one of the costs of current drug policy is the wide-spread abuse of power. If one accepts the fundamental right of humans to equality of opportunity in "life, liberty, and the pursuit of happiness," it is easy to see that power too often prevails abusively in relationships that involve drugs. Police power can intimidate users, even people remotely suspected of being users. Court power can impose sentences grossly disproportionate to the harm inflicted on the public by the possession and personal use of drugs. Prison conditions make possible abuses of institutional power over prisoners and the even more frightening abuses of personal power by brutal prisoners over others. The power of high-level traffickers and "drug barons" over lower-level distributors and street dealers is one of life and death. And overseas we can see evidence of the economic power that the U.S. uses to cause other countries to cooperate in solving America's drug problem, sometimes at the risk of weakening their own institutions and returning their domestic politics to the dominance of the military.

SUMMARY

From this analysis must come the conclusion that the drug problem that plagues America today is indeed tragically costly—in dollars spent for treatment, law enforcement, and incarceration; in dollars lost to sickness, early deaths, lessened productivity, and engagement in non-productive criminal careers; and in dollars spent on efforts to stem the inbound flow of drugs. It is costly in deteriorating neighborhoods, broken families, dead children, corrupt officials, courts that do not administer justice, schools where children cannot learn. Our problem is also costly in degrading the lives and institutions of neighboring countries and in reducing the prospects for good political and economic relations with them.

Yes, the costs are high. Are they less than the value gained? If they are, maybe we should stay on track. If they are not, some major changes are in order. In the next chapter, we will look at how the war on drugs is measuring up to its stated objectives.

Chapter 3

How Effective and How Good a Bargain Is Current Policy?

We have a national drug problem generating costs that can be estimated in dollar terms exceeding $60 billion each year. A cost to the nation of this size demands an accounting of the benefits received in return. To begin this task, let us examine the relationship between what I will call the drug-use cost and the drug-law-enforcement cost. Once this relationship is understood, it becomes easier to deal with the chapter's topical question.

Referring to the 1985 costs calculated by Dorothy Rice and her associates at the University of California–San Francisco and summarized in Table 2.2, the "core costs" of treatment, research, and lost productivity traceable to sickness and early death come to $10.824 billion; these costs arise from drug use. The total of these compares with Rice's category of "other related costs" of $32.461 billion, which derive from the criminal justice system (mainly police, prosecution, private defense, and prisons) and lost productivity of crime victims and the pursuers of criminal careers. Neither of these totals includes federal funds appropriated for efforts to prevent drug use and abuse.

Extrapolation of cost trends and applications of new budget information since 1985 produced 1988 estimates by Rice and her colleagues of $12.896 billion and $42.202 billion for drug-use "core costs" and "other related costs" respectively, for a total of $55.098 billion. These "other related costs" were due almost exclusively to the fact that most drug use is illegal, as represented in Table 2.2. These costs comprise 80 percent of the anti-drug effort as Rice calculated it. The percentage is actually somewhat higher because Rice's figures do not include several hundreds of millions in certain expense categories in the federal budget that are shown in Table 2.3. Put another way, the criminogenic costs of the drug problem are about four times the combined costs of using drugs, treating drug use, and trying to prevent use. I know of no reason to think that the 80 percent ratio of crime-derived costs to the total have changed over the years since 1988, even though total costs have grown markedly since then with inflation both of the dollar and enthusiasm of most of the second drug culture.

How effective is this investment? Are there better ways to use the funds appropriated for the war on drugs? The rest of this chapter takes up the first question. Chapters 5 and 6 will deal with the second.

OBJECTIVES FOR ASSESSMENT

To address this question, one must first establish criteria against which effectiveness can be assessed. There can be no question that the current mix of drug policies in the U.S. is effective. The main problem is in determining which measures of effect one wants to select and defend, and which to reject and deny. By some measures, American policies and their instruments can be acclaimed as successes. Members of the second drug culture—the law enforcers and the coterie of defense lawyers, jail keepers, treatment specialists, prosecutors, urine testers, and others dependent on the drug war—must surely find satisfaction in the constant increases in their budgets, organizations, powers, job security, and career opportunities as the war on drugs continues to escalate. But to note less cynically and more positively—there are several measurable objectives bearing on the general public welfare on whose basis we can assess current and proposed drug policies and their implementing programs.

1. The direct adverse effects on physical and mental health of individual drug users and their families should be reduced, which would imply reductions in both the number of drug users and the individual frequency of use.
2. The quality of neighborhood life and the safety of the streets should be improved. Implications of this objective include fewer dealers on the streets and less violence in the competition for access to the buyers of drugs.
3. The monetary and non-monetary costs to society associated with drug use should be reduced. This objective clearly includes reduced requirements for police officers, court officials, and prisons, as well as the sheer number of persons being arrested, prosecuted, incarcerated, and rendered economically non-productive and more hostile to society as a result.
4. The availability of the services of justice, health, education, and economic opportunity should be enhanced. Concerning justice, this objective includes

not only a reduction of demands on the criminal justice system, but increased overall efficiency of the entire system of justice in handling the range of other business that is now crowded out or postponed by the more urgent criminal cases arising from drug arrests. Access to a reasonable opportunity for health, education, and employment is clearly an aspect of this objective that would apply to all citizens, though most urgently to those most prone to the afflictions of the drug problem as we know it.

5. Economic, political, and cultural relations between the United States and other countries now supplying illegal drugs to the U.S. should become more varied, easier and more profitable.
6. Human rights generally, and civil liberties in particular should be free from infringement by our system of justice.

Note that these criteria emphasize positive objectives and eschew phrases like "clamping down" on traffickers, extraditing "drug barons," "stamping out" drugs, and other hortatory phrases associated with "winning the war on drugs." The development of a successful society that is minimally impeded by drug use must be guided by clearly understandable and measurably attainable goals, not simply by exhortations to stamp out bad things wrought by poorly identified enemies invoked by the metaphor of "the drug war."

Turning now to the assessment of current anti-drug policies and their programs, let us see how they measure up against the criteria stated above.

Physical and Mental Health

There is little direct evidence that can reflect or project trends in the health of drug users and abusers, beyond use or abuse themselves. Bodily afflictions do accompany excessive drug use. As Goldstein and Galant have summarized, it has been found (1) that chronic toxicity from opiates includes disorders of pituitary hormone secretion and hypothalamic function; (2) that alcohol leads to liver damage, brain damage, and pancreatitis; (3) that cocaine can lead to paresthesias (strange tickling sensations of the skin); and (4) that nicotine excesses produce diseases of the circulatory system, peptic ulcers, and other problems.[1] If we accept the premise that abuse is itself a health problem, however, there is a considerable body of evidence to which we can turn. We will sample that evidence, starting with the outcomes of efforts to prevent drug use, and then consider the benefits produced by various treatment programs.

We can start with the reasonable assumption that if the use of harmful substances declines, so also will some of the adverse health effects. The data on drug use are encouraging even if not conclusive. There are signs that the use of marijuana by high school seniors is declining: about 20 percent reported being weekly users in 1989 as compared with 40 percent in 1978. Increasing numbers of high school seniors perceive marijuana to be harmful and disapprove of its use.

Cocaine use has also started to fall, with about 25 percent of adults in an anonymous household survey in 1979 reporting "use in the past year" as compared with 8 percent so reporting in 1990. High school seniors also show declining proportions reporting "use in the past year," from a high of 13 percent in 1985 to 6 percent in 1989.[2] However, it bears repeating that inferences from such surveys must be tempered by knowledge that the high school seniors group cannot include those peers who have dropped out, nor can the household survey include the homeless—and both groups are at higher risk of being attracted to psychoactive drugs. The household survey also omits people living in dormitories, hospitals, jails, prisons, or nursing homes; their absence from the surveyed sample introduces an additional bias.

Surveys done for the National Institute on Drug Abuse (NIDA) have followed high school seniors surveyed earlier into their college years. Questionnaires returned by mail indicate slight but consistent declines in use-in-the-past-year of marijuana, hallucinogens, cocaine, and most other drugs over the four years ending in 1989. The 1200 students in the 1989 sample showed marijuana being used by 33.6 percent, hallucinogens by 5.1 percent, and cocaine by 8.2 percent of those who responded. Alcohol and nicotine use in this sample have remained steady at about 90 percent and 35 percent respectively. Unfortunately, we cannot know how the self-selection in the sample that returned the questionnaires may have biased the resulting data.

One important reason why we cannot be sure that trends in reports of use accurately reflect parallel health trends is that "use" and "abuse" are not the same. Use one time in the last year or the last month or even the last week is usually not enough to produce adverse health effects that can be assigned to a drug; however, use of dirty needles to inject illegal drugs can damage health in one try. Drug-derived health problems are wrought by continued use at higher frequency and intensity than those surveys show.

Another health-related indicator is provided by the Drug Abuse Warning Network (DAWN), which monitors hospital emergency room episodes in which cocaine is mentioned as a corollary. According to reports from the Department of Health and Human Services, records from emergency rooms in ten of the largest American cities show the numbers of mentions going up steadily from 8,831 in 1984 to 43,020 in 1989 as cocaine use expanded, but with signs of a downward turn in the first half of 1990, to a projected annual rate of about 36,000.[3] Mentions for all drugs, including cocaine, decreased from 40,002 in the second quarter of 1988 to 32,985 in the second quarter of 1990. These data, while interesting, do not tell us much about how drugs figured in the events that led people to the emergency rooms—only that there was some evidence of an association of some drug with the person who arrived at the emergency room.

It can reasonably be expected that rate-of-use indicators will not decline a great deal more. For one thing, they are already quite low, and the replacement rate for drop-outs, though unknown, will prevent a dramatic drop toward zero. Another point is that with only moderate use—and most users are moderate by any measure—the seriously unhealthy effects of over-use will be evident only in a relatively small number of people. Also, it is unlikely that the level of drug availability will show significant further drops, short of truly, and unaffordably, draconian measures to interdict suppliers at all levels. Unfortunately, the market indicators of drug availability—supply, demand, and price—have remained fairly stable over the past ten years. Interdiction of foreign drug imports has generally failed to reduce significantly the availability of drugs on the street, according to a study by Peter Reuter of the Rand Corporation.[4] One reason for this is that the original cost of most drugs being imported is so low relative to the potential street price that the shipments interdicted can readily be replaced, thus ensuring a good supply that keeps street prices at affordable levels.

Even though the number of arrests of street dealers tends to go up slowly but steadily over time, there are no good estimates of their replacement rates or of the total number of dealers still doing business.

One must conclude from these reports (and the supporting welter of related data produced for NIDA), even in the face of nearly unavoidable shortcomings in sampling, that drug-war-sponsored educational and propaganda efforts, together with deterrence provided by the risks of getting caught on the wrong side of the law, are resulting in declines in the uses of illicit drugs. Whether or not these declines are truly paralleled by declines in related health problems is more problematic.

Treatment of people to relieve them of drug dependency is being funded at steadily increasing levels, but not as rapidly as prevention programs, and surely not as dramatically as the more aggressive law-enforcement part of the war on drugs. In the next several pages we will consider the effectiveness of treatments in reducing dependency. Later we will look at the relation of the benefits to their costs.

How well do treatment programs work? There is a very general answer: fairly well, and at fairly high cost. But it is more interesting and encouraging to look at the specifics of this complex process. There is a long history of drug treatment and a correspondingly large literature to go with it. Fortunately, in recent years there have been two major reviews of treatment programs, one sponsored by the NIDA and based on data from a national sample of publicly funded programs and written by a team headed by Robert Hubbard.[5] The other was conducted by a team headed by Lawrence Lewin for the Institute of Medicine as mandated by the Anti-Drug Abuse Act of 1986.[6] What follows is a summary of their highlights regarding effectiveness.

By way of introduction, most treatment efforts fall into one of three classes:

First, *outpatient methadone programs* are directed toward heroin abusers. This orally administered synthetic opiate usually produces a day-long relief from the craving for heroin. Maintenance programs are guided by either of two perspectives. One perspective sees heroin abuse as a metabolic problem and seeks to reduce the craving through administering a daily dose of methadone, which is a morphine derivative and a substitute for heroin; social services and psychotherapy are seen as adjuncts to methadone; and abstinence is not a primary goal. From the psychotherapeutic perspective, abuse is seen as a symptom of a major emotional disorder, with methadone as an adjunct to psychotherapy working toward a goal of eventual abstinence from both methadone and heroin.

Second, *therapeutic communities* are twenty-four-hours-a-day residential settings where peer pressure, counseling on interpersonal skills, and psychotherapy aim for a major change in life-style, self perception, and the development of employable skills. Many of these communities operate on the premise that addiction cannot be cured but can be put in remission by a drastic approach to revamping one's style of life, based on a commitment to re-enter society-at-large via the therapeutic subculture. Therapeutic communities are not limited to abusers of any particular drug, but take all comers.

Third, *outpatient drug-free programs* do not involve medication and serve abusers who continue to live in the community. There is great variety in these programs, both as to technique and intensity, and the programs can range from drop-in rap sessions to closely planned and highly structured therapeutic arrangements.

People dependent on heroin (and other opiates) respond well to outpatient methadone programs significantly better than people who are not treated or who are simply detoxified and released. At least one summary report asserts that methadone programs that continue adequate dosages have resulted in successful social rehabilitation of one-half to two-thirds of addicts enrolled, and that reduction in street crime has been well documented.[7] Unsurprisingly, people who stay with the programs longer have better outcomes in terms of drug use and criminal behavior than those who drop out along the way. Methadone maintenance programs are controversial and have been steadily criticized as substituting one opiate for another; there is also some evidence of "leakage" of the medication from approved users to illegal users.

Considering the wider range of drug abusers, therapeutic communities influence clients to use drugs less, to be more socially productive, and to be less criminally inclined. Attrition from treatment communities tends to be high—they get the most difficult cases to begin with—and positive effects are seen with minimal stays of three months, and with further improvement continuing with stays up to eighteen months.

Outpatient drug-free programs, as might be expected from their great variety of clientele and treatments, show the greatest ambiguity in overall results. Clients generally do somewhat better after treatment than before; those who complete treatment do better than drop-outs; retention is poorer than for methadone treatments and therapeutic communities; and effectiveness also varies with intensity of the treatment programs.

In general, something seems to be better than nothing, and this applies to all drugs and general treatment approaches. More encouraging, there seems to be a positive relationship between desired outcomes and the intensiveness and duration of the treatment. But less encouraging is the continuing lack of precision in knowing what kind of treatment will work best with what kind of abuser from what kind of background and whether or not the abuser has a rewarding job. The magic bullet is nowhere in sight. Nevertheless, even in the face of the reservations forced on us by the practically unavoidable shortcomings inherent in the messy nature of clinical research, we have to conclude that treatment as a part of the current policy on drugs has a clearly beneficial effect.

There are still critically important questions we must deal with, however: Do the benefits produced by these treatment programs exceed their costs? And if they do, is the excess large enough to justify continuation of treatment and the research aimed toward improving it? Or should the resources of dollars and talent be shifted to some other part of the effort to reduce the total costs of the drug problem—or even to some altogether different investment in public welfare?

To the first question, the answer is definitely yes. The analysis of treatment reported by Hubbard et al. included calculations of the economic and social costs of drug abuse as a national problem and of the costs of treatment programs. According to the figures, treatment programs when taken all together produce reductions in economic costs. For example, the measure of crime costs to law-abiding citizens per addict (which includes costs to victims, costs of the criminal justice system, and theft), declined from $9,190 one year before treatment to $7,379 one year after treatment.[8] The small difference of $1,811 would have to be produced by treatment costing very little to make a case for treatment being cost-effective.

When the data were analyzed further, however, in order to take into account different lengths of time spent in treatment, the type of treatment given, and other factors related to treatment outcomes, the quality of the treatment investment improved. The revised calculations were based on treatment cost estimates of $18.50 per day in residential settings, and $6.00 for outpatient methadone and outpatient drug-free programs (all of which seem surprisingly low). It was then calculated that each day in residential treatment resulted in an average daily benefit of $33.44 for the time in treatment, yielding a ratio of benefits to costs of 1.81. Reductions in crime-related costs to law-abiding citizens of $37.62 per day during a period (unspecified) after treatment were reported. Counting this reduction as a benefit of treatment yielded a benefit-to-cost ratio of 2.03. The report contained other benefit-to-cost ratios, measuring treatment costs against drug-problem costs to law-abiding citizens and against a broader cost index identified as costs to society, which summarized costs to victims, criminal justice costs, and losses in productivity to crime careers and incarceration. With one exception, all of the benefit-to-cost ratios exceeded 1.00; the lowest was .92 and the highest, 4.28.[9]

Based on this study of a national sample of ten thousand clients in publicly funded treatment programs, the Hubbard group concludes that treatment pays off—that there are substantial reductions in crime-related and other costs both during and following treatment, that the reduction appears to be at least as large as the cost of the treatment, that much of the expenditure is recovered during the time of treatment, and that the return on investment in general continues for at least a year after leaving treatment. "The modest investment of $5,000 for a year of outpatient drug-free or methadone treatment and $15,000–20,000 a year for residents in therapeutic communities will produce benefits that far outweigh the costs. It is also more prudent to invest in treatment rather than pay the

$10,000–25,000 annual costs of incarceration or the $80,000 in medical costs for each AIDS patient." The report of the group sponsored by the Institute of Medicine is affirmative about the general value of treatment, but is much less sanguine about the return on investment. The report notes that very few benefit/cost studies have been conducted, and those that have been were derived from fully controlled clinical trials, and thus were freed from much of the measurement error that would exist in broader assessments.

Both sets of conclusions leave the answer to the second and third questions posed earlier decidedly up in the air. Does the excess of benefit over cost justify continuance of treatment and supporting research, or should the resources be put somewhere else? In my view, the ratios of benefit to costs are mostly irrelevant: so long as they give some assurance of return and approximate 1.00, we can be assured that a public good is being enhanced. Bigger ratios are better than small ones, to be sure, and the array of such ratios can tell us where to make additional treatment investments and which kinds of treatment might benefit from further research.

Finally, let's not forget that one feature of the drug war, broadly conceived, is the range of treatment programs that have been developed and made available at public expense for drug abusers, some more effective than others, but on the whole a fairly positive process.

Quality of Neighborhood Life

It is hard to criticize current drug policy for failing to maintain neighborhood quality and safety of the streets, for it has not been an explicit objective of such policy until relatively recently, and then because the drug-war-induced violence required it. The objective of making streets and neighborhoods safe from crime has been embodied in various pieces of federal crime control legislation, such as the Omnibus Crime Control and Safe Streets Act of 1968[10] and several subsequent crime control bills including the Crime Control Act of 1990.[11] All of these have anti-drug provisions. Thus the war on drugs can claim a role in the effort to make streets safe and livable, even though the war's main thrust is to stamp out drug use and drug-related crime. Thus we have an interesting paradox: the drug war has a mission to eliminate the street crime and the other neighborhood problems that it has created.

Much of street violence is connected with the drug trade. Since there are no protections through the courts against unfair trade practices in the illicit drug industry, more direct means of protecting or expanding market share are used. From drug warriors, we understandably hear calls for action to return safety to the streets and halt neighborhood deterioration by stamping out trade in drugs. True, if there were no drug traders in a neighborhood, its streets would be much safer. As we shall see in the Chapter 4 summary of New York City's efforts to stamp out drugs in selected neighborhoods, heavy policing, often combined with grass-roots community support, can clean up neighborhoods and make the streets safe and enjoyable. One mere practical problem is the effort's high cost. Another is the pop-up effect: neighborhood clamp-downs do not eliminate demand; they mainly redirect supply. Thus, drug trade suppressed in one area pops up in another, leaving the net effect on drug availability close to zero.

Still, one cannot fault present policy and its implementing programs for lack of effort. A review by John Martin shows declines in personal victimization crime rates from 1975 to 1986, with rape, robbery, and burglary going down by 25.5 percent, 24 percent, and 11.4 percent, respectively.[12] In contrast is a 43 percent increase in drug-related arrests from 1977 to 1987, followed by another 43 percent rise in the single year ending in December 1988. A report from the Drugs and Crime Clearinghouse summarizes total estimated arrests for drug abuse violations (not specifically defined) for the ten years 1980 through 1989 to be rising steadily from 580,900 to 1,361,700.[13] These figures themselves do not say much about violent street crime and turf wars, but it can be assumed that arrests for offenses involving violence were in parallel ascendency over the periods of these reports.

Drug-related crimes appear to have become a top priority for law enforcement. Have street safety and neighborhood quality been significantly improved overall by the law enforcement efforts? The answer must remain that we do not really know. Has the overall effect of official policy and the war on drugs been to produce safer streets? No.

Economic and Social Costs

There is clear evidence that drug-related monetary costs to society have continued to rise. Federal funds authorized for the war on drugs, including funds for prevention, treatment, and research, rose from $1.5 billions in fiscal year 1981 to $6.4 billions in 1988 to $10.5 billions in 1991, an average increase of 391 percent.[14] If one excludes funds for prevention, treatment, and research—investments with higher potential for contributing to the public good—the average rate of increase in federal authorizations for the drug war goes to 471 percent because prevention, treatment, and research are targeted for decreasing proportions of federal appropriations. President Bush requested a total of $11.7 billion for 1992. Thus the drug war—supported by the second and third drug cultures (as these are described in chapter 1)—appears to continue as a powerful machine for generating and spending tax dollars.

Non-monetary costs to society are harder to trace. Expanded and improved treatment and prevention might be cutting personal pain and losses of productive time experienced by users and abusers. But such gains may well be offset by the increasing loads and decreasing efficiency in the justice system and by the continuing infringements of civil liberties resulting from the urgency with which the law-enforcement component of the war is prosecuted.

Social Service Institutions

It is hard to assign an overall grade to the contributions of current policy to the services of justice, health, education, and economic opportunity, because such contributions have not been policy objectives in the drug war. One could argue that the costs of the drug war drain resources that could be assigned to various human development programs, but there is no particular reason to believe that were the drug war to be cancelled any particular human development alternative would see increased funding. The costs to the system of justice as we have described them in Chapter 2 can generally be seen as undesirable. And a cynic could say that tremendous economic opportunities have come to a large number of young people in the form of very high-paying jobs in the illicit drug market.

National drug policy has not been absent from the education business either, and several good publications for school use have been produced, such as *How Drugs Can Affect Your Life*[15] and *Drugs, Society, and Human Behavior.*[16] However, a lot of people disagree with the merits of other aspects of drug education. While no one questions the need for good programs in the schools that are directed toward getting kids to cut down on drug use, there is reasonable concern about the balance of drug-education programs (they do not have nearly as much to say about nicotine and alcohol) and particularly about the credibility of the emphasis on scare tactics. High school students I have talked with recognize that there is a real risk in using drugs, but they report that a lot of the material presented is laughable and not worth taking seriously—the "brains-frying-in-the-skillet" advertisement is especially scoffworthy. That this attitude may undermine the value of the more credible stuff should be taken seriously by the drug educators.

On balance, national drug policy scores poorly on this criterion of enhancement of human development services, and is redeemed from failure by the drug treatment programs that not only do their own kind of good, but provide additional health screening and access to treatments of other afflictions.

International Relations

Here again drug warriors can claim immunity from charges of failure, since improving foreign relations has not been part of their mandate; however, Elliot Abrams, Assistant Secretary of State for Latin American Affairs in the Reagan administration, claims that democratic leaders throughout the western hemisphere share the American view that "sustaining democracy and battling the narco-terrorist threat are inextricably linked." Former Attorney General Edwin Meese III and New York's former mayor Ed Koch have argued the benefits of using U.S. military means to take part in cutting off the northward drug traffic. Other writers take a sharply different view of the situation that has developed in relation to a number of Latin American countries. In Chapter 2, we reviewed some of the heavy costs imposed on several Latin American countries by our drug war.

To get a flavor of official U.S. attitudes about how such countries should perform and how these attitudes are translated into conditions imposed on countries if they are to receive economic bounties from the United States, it is interesting to look at just a few of the provisions of the Anti-Drug Abuse Act of 1986.[17] The law

1. restores half of planned assistance to Bolivia *if* the President of the United States certifies that Bolivia has cooperated with U.S. narcotics interdiction operations that have resulted in a significant disruption of the industry;
2. conditions restoration of full assistance to Bolivia on our President's certification that Bolivia met its (coca plant) eradication targets for 1985 or agreed to meet 1985 targets in 1987 and is judged as progressing well toward 1985 targets;
3. withholds $1 million of narcotics control assistance to Mexico *unless* the President reports to Congress that Mexico has fully investigated and tried the people responsible for the murder of U.S. Drug Enforcement Administration (DEA) agent Enrique Camarena and the torture of DEA agent Victor Cortez; and
4. expresses the sense of the Congress that *unless* Mexico shows substantial progress in the matters of DEA agents Camarena and Cortez, and in Mexican

> efforts in interdiction or eradication of drugs and reducing cross-border trafficking, the U.S. president should consider some punitive actions against Mexico—actions that have nothing to do with the drug problem. One such action recommended is issuing a mandatory travel advisory—which would seriously damage Mexico's tourism industry. Other recommendations would be restriction of economic assistance and denial of favorable American votes in development banks such as the International Monetary Fund.

There are other recommendations in the 1986 Act, and the Anti-Drug Abuse Act of 1988[18] continues these and adds still more. But this sample should show the potential of American policy for offending other countries toward which we claim to have otherwise friendly intentions. Mexicans I have interviewed express dismay over their country's having to play such a big part in the U.S. drug war when they have so relatively minor a problem with drug abuse at home; with resignation they see this as just another difficulty in living so closely with "el gigante del norte."

Particularly offensive to Mexicans was the June 1992 ruling by the U.S. Supreme Court that the kidnapping for trial in the United States of a Mexican citizen suspected by our DEA of participating in the 1985 killing of its agent Enrique Camarena was constitutionally and legally correct on the grounds that the extradition treaty between the two countries does not explicitly bar such kidnapping. The Mexican government responded by shutting down cooperation with the U.S. drug war in Mexico. According to a *New York Times* analysis, the door may now be open for similar kidnappings in other countries.[19] Not only that, other countries may now find it tempting to kidnap Americans within the United States in order to try them in their own countries.

Overall, then, one cannot credit the war on drugs, which is the manifestation of U.S. drug policy most evident from outside our borders, with improving relations with other countries.

Related to this criterion is a still broader one—the effects of American leadership in pressing for a tough anti-drug stance by countries throughout the world. Does maintaining high world-wide prices of drugs, and hence an attractive market for traffickers, increase the risk of strife in countries far from our own homeland? I think it would be foolish to deny this. In an interview with a Drug Enforcement Administration officer in Ankara, Turkey, I asked if the international drug traffic was financing the Kurdish terrorist group PKK in their repeated efforts to force Turkey to give the once-nomadic Kurds a permanent homeland. He replied that DEA intelligence sources had established beyond a reasonable doubt that PKK agents in Lebanon were bankrolling much of that effort through large-scale trading in illegal drugs.

On a much grander scale are the effects of American efforts to control the international drug trade or to use it in the service of U.S. military or other foreign relations objectives. These have been described in fascinating detail in Alfred McCoy's 1972 classic *The Politics of Heroin in Southeast Asia* and his recent expanded second edition, *The Politics of Heroin: CIA Complicity in the Global Drug Trade*. Far too extensive to be summarized here, McCoy's analysis concludes that "since the United States first prohibited narcotics use in the early 1920s, succeeding administrations have used repressive strategies that share one essential attribute—failure." McCoy explains this common fate largely on the basis of American unwillingness to participate fully in the League of Nations' gradual but effective attempts to reduce the world's supply of narcotics after World War I. The U.S. assumed more leadership in the United Nations after World War II, but then abandoned the multilateral approach in favor of more active bilateral efforts targeted at specific sources of supply. McCoy sums up the certainty of continued failure:

> Simply put, narcotics are major global commodities resistant to any attempt at localized suppression. As long as the demand for drugs in First World cities continues to grow, Third World producers will find a way to supply their markets. Ignoring these simple economic realities, the United States has, over the past seventy years, applied localized tactics to deal with a global problem. Before World War II, FBN [Federal Bureau of Narcotics] agents tried to eradicate America's illicit narcotics supply by pursuing drug dealers inside the United States, ignoring the world market that delivered the heroin. After the war, FBN agents began operating abroad with the police of individual countries, seeking a localized interdiction of drug shipments to America from Marseilles or Mexico. . . . Even if Bush's massive military effort wipes out the entire Andean cocaine trade, Asia's opium farmers are already producing record harvests. The heroin exporters of Pakistan and Burma stand ready to fill the void in the U.S. drug market that might appear when cocaine supplies slacken.[20]

Human Rights and Civil Liberties

The protection of civil liberties is never a specific objective of a crime prevention program, even though the program is expected to operate within constitutional constraints on ferocity. This is normal and understandable since it is the duty of the criminal justice system to find, arrest, and bring to trial people who are suspected of doing bad things. Fighting crime is seen as a universal good and bringing the "bad guys" to justice is what gets rewarded. And fighting especially noxious crime may encourage further enthusiasm in tracking down suspects and putting civil liberties and rights at increased risk. In defense of the police, one should understand that much of anti-drug law enforcement is fraught with danger of serious injury or death; therefore, in spite of intentions to respect the rights of suspicious persons, police are sure to make mistakes and take actions that in retrospect may have violated constitutional rights.

Attorney Eric Sterling has reviewed drug-related legislation and court cases relating to each of the first ten amendments to the U.S. Constitution and finds offenses against all of them; major examples were summarized in Chapter 2 as components of the drug problem's cost.[21] Some of Sterling's claims may seem a bit far fetched, like the assertion that government-mandated urine testing is today's equivalent of quartering troops in homes (Third Amendment) because Tuesday's drug test could reveal that a person smoked marijuana in his home last Saturday night, just "as if the king's soldier were sitting there in the living room." But most of his summary rests on well-known cases and all of his examples remind us of the possibility for spreading rights-abuse in the zealous pursuit of drug abuse.

Sterling uses the relatively non-controversial Ninth Amendment as the basis for concern over human rights in general. These rights, he asserts, are rooted in the statement that "the enumeration in the Constitution of certain rights shall not be construed to deny or disparage others retained by the people," those that derive from the principle that "we are endowed by our Creator with certain inalienable rights." From here one can go on to the argument (to be developed further in Chapter 6) that one has a right to ownership of, and control over, one's own body, a right that is sternly denied by the mountain of legislation that declares and sustains the war on drugs.

The Anti-Drug Abuse Act of 1986 established a set of mandatory sentences for certain drug law violations, a set that not only deprives judges of discretionary authority in sentencing, but permits the coercive abuse of plea bargaining in ways that amount to depriving a person of "life, liberty, or property without due process of law" (a Fifth Amendment erosion). A prosecutor can warn an offender: "If you go to trial on this first offense as charged and lose, you will get a mandatory ten years, possibly more. But if you plead guilty to this lesser offense, included in the charge, I will recommend a much lower sentence." In situations like this, the guilty plea is coerced, and the offender goes to jail without trial.

Some might ask, so what if a few "minor" constitutional breeches are committed? The law breakers are being jailed and society is the better for it, right? Wrong! The Bill of Rights is the backbone of every individual liberty that we have enjoyed these many years, and to allow any one of those rights to be violated and eroded for any cause, however virtuous that cause might seem, is to risk a loss of liberty for everyone. In the civil liberties arena, the war on drugs has lived up to the assertion that it is not so much a war on drugs as a war on people and that as in all wars many of the casualties are blameless victims and the basic rights of everyone.

SUMMARY

The judgment of the success or failure of any policy or program derives from the standards set for it. American policy on illicit drugs seems to be having success if measured against arrests, convictions, imprisonments, seizures, or property forfeitures as prescribed and permitted under the law. Such measures as these, however, are indicators of activity directed at a problem rather than of how the problem itself—in terms of public health and safety—is being changed. When measured against actual effects on public health, the successes seem less grand but are probably coming about. Efforts to prevent the use of illicit drugs are reflected in declines in reported drug use, in drugs mentioned in connection with hospital emergency room episodes, and in rises in the perception of drug use as dangerous; these are all moves in the right direction, even taking into account errors of sampling and measurement and the tendency of drug warriors to exaggerate their successes. Treatment efforts are producing modest but steady retrievals of drug abusers from the worst effects of abuse and are well worth the return on public investment.

On other measures, drug policy does not seem to be doing as well. Drug-related arrests continue apace; drug availability remains high and prices low; inner city streets remain hazardous; relations with drug-supplying countries are, if changing at all, changing for the worse; and civil liberties of Americans continue to erode as the enthusiasm of the drug warriors and the tolerance of spectators rise.

Where and how do we go from here? In the next chapter, we will take the assumption that the illegal status of marijuana, heroin, cocaine, and their derivatives will continue in effect. Then we ask, What can be done to beef up the war on drugs and what would be the likely consequences of staying tough in the criminal orientation?

Chapter 4

Policy Options Within the Criminalization Context

The preceding chapter reviewed the available information on the effectiveness of current policy and practice in reducing the impact of illicit drugs. Our conclusion was that by a number of measures, such as arrests, quantity of would-be imported drugs seized, and assets of drug law violators confiscated, significant progress has been realized over the several years of the Reagan-Bush administrations and their drug wars. We also concluded that by other measures, including the number of actual users, the amount of drugs sold on the street, the quality of neighborhood life, the damage of the economies and political institutions of several friendly countries, and a number of other measures of economic and social costs, the war on drugs was making little or no progress—in fact was presiding over a situation that is worsening in several ways.

Policy being slow to change, and the people and institutions invested in it the same, we can expect that current practice will be continued as long as significant opposition is lacking. It is not surprising that the commanders in the drug war believe that the war might be winnable if sufficient additional resources were made available to them—the policy is okay, we just need more capacity to implement it.

As a way to appreciate the feasibility of policies and practices alternative to those now being pursued, it may be helpful to examine the consequences of trying to push current anti-drug practices to their limits. We will do this by imagining what it would be like first to maximize efforts to reduce the supply of drugs, and then to maximize efforts to reduce demand—all within the current context of the sale and use of drugs being largely illegal activities.

MAXIMAL EFFORTS TO REDUCE SUPPLY

The simplest solution to any problem of doing wrong is to make unavailable the means for wrongdoing, be they guns, brass knuckles, switchblade knives, burglary tools, or illegal drugs.

Cutting Off External Sources

There are two general ways of reducing the supply of drugs from the outer world: one is to persuade exporting countries to reduce the cultivation of crops from which drugs are produced and to stop the refinement and exportation of the finished product; the other is to interdict the transit of drugs that elude those countries' efforts to stop them.

The difficulties with the first of these were revealed again in news reports of the San Antonio drug summit of February 1992.[1] President Bush urged the Latin American presidents to do more to curtail drug production, but he was unable to offer additional financial help either to bolster the on-the-ground effort or to develop alternative sources of foreign trade. Several leaders expressed concern about armies strengthened by anti-drug monies becoming threats to civilian governments. President Fujimori of Peru argued against targets calling for rapid cuts in coca production because of the serious disruption they would wreak on his already weak economy. At least five of the national leaders called for more investment in their countries that could create jobs for the thousands of coca farmers who could become victims of success in a continuing drug war. All told, the meeting appears to have produced more ceremony than substance and to have signalled an end to the U.S. administration's hope for a major cut-back in the Latin American supply.

Interdiction continues as an attractive effort to seal our borders against the entry of illegal drugs. Clearly it would be possible to increase the amount of air and sea surveillance over ships and planes suspected of bringing illegal drugs to our shores. Peter Reuter has shown that from 1981 to 1985 seizures of in-bound cocaine rose from 1.7 percent to 25 percent of estimated shipments.[2] The cost of this process of interdiction was planned at about $2.2 billion dollars in fiscal year 1993 under the president's budget proposal.

If one optimistically assumes that the 25 percent interdiction rate would go to 35 percent by 1993 and also assumes a high correlation between interdiction efforts and the percent of in-bound drugs captured, we might guess (generously, I fear) that adding another $2.2 billion worth of people and equipment maintaining surveillance and otherwise pursuing interdiction would raise the seizure rate to about 70 percent. A continued interdiction effort of this magnitude would doubtless please the Coast Guard by providing an expanding horizon of career development, and it would go some distance toward ensuring activity for military units whose missions are shrinking along with the cold war.

Extrapolation of trends can be risky to hopes for a reasonable conclusion, however, for the relationship between tonnages seized and the cost of seizing cannot be expressed in a straight line showing a steady relationship between interdiction efforts and seizures. The fact is that seizure costs per ton go up as smugglers become more ingenious and the price of producing the raw material goes down. Reuter reports a simple example: In fiscal year 1978, the average Coast Guard seizure of marijuana was ten metric tons; in fiscal year 1986 it was five tons.[3] The reduced size of shipment lowered the risk of seizure for each ton and apparently doubled the per ton cost of seizure, since the cost of stopping and searching a vessel remained at best the same, regardless of the amount of the drug carried. Reuter's analysis further shows that the greatest effect on drug price occurs through the system of distribution *after* the drug has sucessfully entered the United States, simply because it is so cheap to produce drugs in source countries: it is as easy for the system to replace ten kilograms of cocaine in Bolivia as to replace one kilogram in Detroit. All in all, interdiction is not a cost-effective way of raising the price of cocaine and reducing its availability on the street.

But even assuming a greatly expanded interdiction effort, whence would come the costs in a stagnant or slowly growing economy? Clearly, the contest between interest groups, each claiming to represent the public good, would confuse or stifle so grand an expansion of active interdictive efforts.

Closing Off Normal Ports of Entry

Interdiction might also be aided by intensifying the searching of commercial packages at the regular ports of entry. Who knows what Thai drug dealer may have managed to insert 500 grams of heroin into each Panasonic videocassette recorder in a shipment coming from Japan? Or tucked cocaine into the doors of Hyundais from Korea? No one can know without a search. Perhaps the Japanese and Koreans would be willing to do the inspecting for us at their plants, for a charge?

And Americans returning from abroad could plan an extra day for participating in the great inspection of all luggage and parcels accompanying them, unless the Customs Service could somehow increase eightfold its inspection force and buildings or discover a fool proof way of detecting illegal drugs without opening parcels and suitcases. Not very likely.

The sheer impracticality of inspecting a significant proportion of goods entering through customs is revealed in the number of potential carriers of smuggled goods. A U.S. Customs Service report of entries requiring Customs Service surveillance for 1988 shows more than five million containers entering over land and more than three million by sea. Then there are slightly more than one hundred million automobiles with more than three hundred million passengers and more than 54 million passengers coming in by air.[4] Need we go on?

In real life, we have already had one bad experience in this area—back in 1969 with Mexico. President Richard Nixon had become exasperated with the Mexican government's complaints to the effect that the American drug problem was a problem made in America, not in Mexico. He was easily persuaded by his attorney general, John Mitchell, to "close the border," and on September 21, "Operation Intercept" began. From the Pacific Ocean to the Gulf of Mexico, U.S. Customs officials scrutinized every pedestrian and every vehicle crossing the border into the United States. The army set up mobile radar units between San Diego and El Paso, and three additional airplanes were rented to intensify the search for inbound carriers of contraband from Sonora.

The result was calamitous. In Tijuana, sixteen lanes of traffic backed up trying to make it to the gateway to California. Mexican vegetables rotted in the heat as their trucks idled. Mexicans with permits to work in the United States could not go to their jobs. Money spent in Mexico by American visitors dropped by as much as 70 percent in one border town or another. The effects were felt on the American side as well. Mexicans stopped crossing the border to shop, unwilling to undergo the indignity of the questioning and the searching of handbags. The absence of significant drug busts brought derision on the whole operation, but intercepting drugs had not really been the main objective of the scheme; its unannounced purpose was to put the heat on the Mexicans to do more themselves to stop the northward flow of drugs.

Finally, after seventeen days of confusion, insult, and hostility on both sides of the border, President Diaz Ordaz sent his deputy attorney general to Washington to negotiate an end to the border searches. After much angry talk, a compromise was struck: Operation Intercept would cease, and the Mexicans would agree to a joint enterprise, called Operation Cooperation, in which American agents would be stationed in Mexico with authority to search for poppy and marijuana fields, and the Mexicans would start a program to try to stop the marijuana trade.

All told, the costs of Operation Intercept on both sides of the border, while not large monetarily, did cost the United States dearly in Mexican respect and willingness to cooperate in other ways. About the only benefit to emerge was the understanding by the American administration that even a marginally successful interdiction program at our borders was beyond American power to sustain it.[5]

Another possibility, one that would not create confusion at Mexican-American border crossings, would be to build an impenetrable fence from San Diego to Brownsville, complete with watch towers, lights, and guards. But how offensive do we want to be toward an economically important neighbor with whom we are trying to establish new trade policies? And which U.S. government programs should give up the $1.5 billion of capital cost[6] and forty million dollars in annual operating costs for such protection?

Aside from physical interdictions of incoming drugs, it might be possible to increase appropriations for foreign aid to countries that produce and export illegal drugs in our direction. This money could then be used to induce these countries to cut back on growing and refining the products we would like to keep out, or to invite our army into their countries to "help them" stamp out the trade. This kind of activity, as noted in Chapters 2 and 3, has proved unpopular in countries where it has been tried and has not begun to compensate their economies for the losses in hard international currencies that these cooperative efforts have cost them. Do we really want to go to such extremes, risking broad-based offense to nationalist attitudes and endangering other American interests in these countries? The short summary in Chapter 2 of the Colombian experience should be instructive. Only if we could find success in helping the drug-producing countries to develop other sources of legitimate agricultural trade could we expect this approach to work—and then brace for the outcry from American producers of the foods that would then be competing with theirs in the world market.

Direct Military Incursions into Drug-Supplying Countries

Vincent Bugliosi has seriously offered the rather extreme proposition that the United States should mount a military search-and-find operation within Colombia "by that number of American military personnel deemed necessary by the Joint Chiefs of Staff to accomplish the job." Speaking of drug lords, Bugliosi argues that we should "make each of them realize the high probability (not possibility) that if they continue they will pay with their lives. . . . " He continues, "If, for whatever reason, the Colombian government would not authorize our military intervention, then we should intervene without their blessing."[7] He argues that the Posse Comitatus law, which began as an amendment to the Army Appropriations Act of 1878 and which restricts the use of the military forces in enforcing domestic criminal laws, would not apply in this case. He cites as legitimating precedents miscellaneous presidential military initiatives, among them the recent invasions of Grenada and Panama. Bugliosi does not examine the international complications that would necessarily follow from such a high-handed pursuit of American interests.

Stopping Internal Flows of Drugs

Turning now to the domestic scene, let us examine the feasibility of maximizing efforts to get in the way of delivering drugs within our borders. The most obvious first step would be to put enough more police on the streets to interfere with the trading by local customers and dealers. How many would it take, and how much would it cost? It would vary greatly from place to place, with the busier markets requiring many more police than those in smaller and less busy markets, but New York City's experience with Operation Pressure Point (OPP) 1 in the mid-1980s gives clues as to what to expect.[8] OPP-1 was launched in 1984 on the Lower East Side where "gentrification" of an area with run-down commercial buildings, dilapidated housing, and a high proportion of minorities resulted in strong pressures on the New York police department (NYPD) to break up street-level drug traffic. Uniformed NYPD officers on foot made searches and arrests and questioned people suspected of being sellers or buyers. Police of the housing and transit authorities intensified their patrols in housing projects and the subways. "Buy and bust" operations by the police narcotics division were expanded.

By September 1989, about 2000 days into the operation, about 36,000 arrests had been made for narcotics offenses, out of a total of nearly 47,000 arrests in the area. Trafficking in the target area was noticeably down as were drug-related property crimes, and the rate of gentrification of the protected neighborhood increased. Michael Letwin, president of the Association of Legal Aid Attorneys, concluded after studying the records behind the OPP-1 reports that the decline in drug dealing was more apparent than real: drug activity in the OPP-1 zone became more covert, moved off the streets and indoors, and was displaced to poorer parts of the neighborhood and into other neighborhoods. Yes, increased street-level traffic control can reduce trafficking at the points where overt police action takes place. Regrettably, the suppression of the drug trade in one neighborhood leads to its popping up in others.

Similar results came from another New York City drug-control effort, the Tactical Narcotics Team (TNT) program, which was an elaborate arrangement involving twenty-three city agencies. The TNT strategy was to have teams saturate an area for thirty to ninety days, performing "buy and bust" operations, and then be replaced by a smaller team as the larger effort moved to another neighborhood. As with the OPP-1 experience, the TNT program produced large numbers of arrests, reduced dealing in target areas, increased dealing in adjacent areas, demonstrated ready replacement of arrested dealers, and resulted in an all-around effect on drug abuse approximating zero.

In the fiscal year 1989, New York City spent nearly a billion dollars on drug-related law enforcement; police, courts, jails, probation, legal aid, were the major costs. About $116 million was spent on the TNT program from 1988 to 1990. All of this money represents a commitment of "more resources to the war on drugs than any other municipality," according to then Police Chief Benjamin Ward.

Few cities can afford this level of intensity in efforts to control street-level drug dealing, even with strong federal support via the Drug Enforcement Administration and the federal court system. The results of New York's battles in this war should counsel against further and more intensive experiments unless they are committed to a long-time operation and coupled closely with community based anti-drug groups.

Community Mobilization

Because it is dramatic and deeply motivated by drawing on the disgust of neighborhood citizen groups, community mobilization can have definite effects on the drug supply. This is especially true when the action is backed by police.[9] Harassing dealers and crack houses sends a strong message that is often heeded when it is sustained, forcing dealers to move to other less hostile areas. Despite its virtues, community mobilization has some drawbacks. It is hard to sustain and is likely to be ineffective without steady police participation, which of necessity is limited. Furthermore, it exposes citizens to the risk of being killed in direct confrontations. It also offers citizens the temptation to vigilantism with its attendant dangers to innocent people, as well as to cavalier attitudes toward law and order.

Random Searches

In addition to "buy and bust" operations and deterrence through massive police presence, one might also reduce the delivery of contraband through more intense searches of bags and parcels of virtually anyone in a situation where there may be a lot of drugs being transported. Though such seemingly random searches and seizures have long been contested as violations of citizens' Fourth Amendment protections, the practice is nonetheless followed more often than we should like. It is likely to become even more frequent given recent trends of the judiciary to develop reasons for negating the "exclusionary rule," which since 1914 has protected the public from violations of Fourth Amendment protections "against unreasonable searches and seizures." A recent example of this practice is the Bostick case, in which the Supreme Court struck down a Florida court ruling that personal searches in a group wherein one or more persons were thought to be transporting drugs was "inherently coercive" and hence unconstitutional. Terrance Bostick was confronted on a bus by several police officers and gave permission, after being asked, for a bag he was carrying to be searched. Drugs were discovered in a second bag and Bostick was arrested and convicted, but later appealed successfully, claiming that the consent to the search was coerced. The Florida Supreme Court held the sheriff's practice of "working the buses" to be unconstitutional, that a reasonable person would not have felt free to leave the bus to avoid police questioning. On review, the U.S. Supreme Court reversed the Florida court's decision, holding that a consensual encounter does not trigger Fourth Amendment scrutiny. In his dissent, Justice Thurgood Marshall said that suspicionless police sweeps of buses "bear all the indicia of coercive and unjustified intrusion associated with the general warrant."[10] A recent review of five Fourth Amendment cases in the Supreme Court's 1990 term (four of them concerned drug related charges) concludes that the Court showed a narrowing view of Fourth Amendment protections and a tendency to defer in favor of law enforcement interests.[11] Even though the Supreme Court may conclude that searches like Bostick's and broad sweeps of groups that may include drug law offenders are not "inherently coercive," they nonetheless contribute to criminalizing a population and further damaging a neighborhood's quality of life.

Stricter Penalties

Making penalties for trafficking more severe is another tempting proposition. As one example, William Rusher of the *Washington Times* has advocated the death penalty "for anyone involved in the commercial sale of drugs."[12] As reported by Steven Jonas, William Bennett, President Bush's first "drug czar," took a typically more dramatic position on "The Larry King Show" of June 15, 1989:

> CALLER: My question is to Mr. Bennett. Why build prisons? Get tough like Arabia. Behead the damn drug dealers. We're just too darn soft.
>
> BENNETT: It's actually—there's an interesting point. One of the things that I think is a problem is that we are not doing enough that is morally proportional to the nature of the offense. I mean, what the caller suggests is morally plausible. Legally, it's difficult. But say—
>
> LARRY KING: Behead?
>
> BENNETT: Yeah. Morally I don't have any problem with that.

Mandatory and non-appealable death sentences for all drug offense convictions might deter attempts to deliver drugs to customers—if they were truly enforced, which they obviously could not be, unless the courts allow serious erosion of the Eighth Amendment's prohibitions of cruel and unusual punishment. But even constitutionally acceptable sentences stricter than those now on the books would hugely increase court and incarceration costs and in the fairly short run probably not make much difference in the drug market. As Michael Letwin summarizes, "No matter how harsh, the criminal justice system's sanctions are still less deadly than the well-known occupational hazards that inner-city youth in the drug trade accept as the price of unparalleled opportunity for money, prestige, and power."[13]

Reducing the Relative Attractiveness of Drug-Related Careers

Another method for reducing the supply of drugs to customers would be to make alternative career opportunities available to dealers so attractive that dealerships might go begging. Students of the drug problem are unanimous in their view that the financial and social status rewards of drug dealing for young inner-city youths are so attractive relative to the low-paying alternatives as to provide a steady supply of dealers to replace those arrested or killed. Were this supply to be reduced by the availability of better and less dangerous career opportunities, not only would the drug problem—whether conceived as a criminal or public health issue—be significantly reduced, but personal development opportunities and national productivity would also be materially enhanced.

What would this cost? This potential solution to the supply problem is extremely complex and contains so many obstacles of a social and cultural nature, in addition to the sheer number of dollars needed to provide training for alternative careers, as to defy cost calculations. One could start with estimates of job training costs based on technical school and junior college education. The annual operating costs per student of a vocational-technical education at the secondary level preparing people for entry level jobs in carpentry, plumbing, electricity, among other fields, comes to about $6000 as an overall average. A two-year junior college education, leading to an associate degree and skills in various well-paying crafts, like engineering aide, cabinet maker, electronics technician, and automobile mechanic, would cost about $6650 in tuition and subsistence, according to studies by the College Entrance Examination Board. Multiplying these amounts by an (under-) estimate 20,000 youthful drug dealers nation-wide produces an approximate total of around $133 mililion to put these people through two years of schooling.

Aside from the mere practical matter of money, however, the far more formidable problem seems to be to provide incentives for young people otherwise attracted to drug dealing to take time off from the drug trades to attend school at all. There exist no solid data that would provide the basis for estimating what these incentives might be or what they might cost—other than the wildest speculation based on the earnings that would have to be foregone by giving up the drug business to attend school—probably at least $50,000 per former dealer–now student. The often cited example that it costs as much to keep a youthful offender in a state "reform school" for a single year as to put her through a good four-year college draws support from no one as a guide for rehabilitating the offender. Even given the possible reduction in the long-term cost of the national drug problem that might be realized through applying such attractive educational incentives, people are understandably unwilling to reward criminals by buying them expensive educations. As we have said, Americans are given to the quick solution to problems of all kinds, and this potential solution would be neither quick nor certain.

CONTROLLING DEMAND

Now we turn to the other force that drives the market for illegal drugs: What, within the context of the policy of prohibition and criminalization, might be done to limit demand?

Voluntary Treatment

Treatment opportunities for current drug users could be materially expanded in the hope of reducing the number of customers for the drug merchant. At present we spend nearly $2 billion on treatment and treatment-related research in both public and private facilities. This compares with around $7 billion for alcohol abusers, who are about four times more numerous.

In the total arithmetic of drug-problem costs, treatment costs are relatively small, and one could argue for a greater investment in this effort. But as our discussion in Chapter 3 showed, a major expansion of treatments within the current state of the arts would very likely effect a reduction in the number of drug users and abusers, but not enough to make a significant dent in the overall demand for presently illegal drugs. And such a modest prospect could not generate the political support needed for a massive expansion of treatment programs. Treating and healing are just not as dramatic as warring and punishing.

Involuntary Treatment

In the eyes of people who view drug abuse as an illness, drug users currently in jails and prisons make up an attractive population to be required to undergo programs designed to reduce their needs for illegal drugs. Indeed some such programs already exist, but they have not been systematically evaluated and their effectiveness remains unknown. Psychological or psychiatric treatments in such settings suffer the distinct and pervasive risk of failure for all such treatments: the person being treated has to strongly desire to abandon the behavior patterns at issue and be expected to seek an environment that will sustain the changes wrought by the treatment. These conditions are not common in prison populations, which exist involuntarily and many of whose members will probably return on release to settings more likely to support connections with illegal drugs than to discourage them. Drug users returning from prison, even after treatment, are not likely to contribute a measurable reduction in the demand for drugs, nor to a reduction in the work force that supplies the drug-consuming market.

Involuntary Testing

Requiring urine tests as a condition for obtaining or holding jobs is frequently proposed, especially for jobs in which poor performance is suspected of posing a risk to public health and safety. Several thousand firms now do this. Murray Jarvik has suggested saliva testing as preferable to urine testing "because saliva can be collected under direct observation without embarrassment or pain."[14] He suggests also some innovative approaches to testing in communities with high levels of drug abuse such as to offer free state lottery tickets to people who agree to undergo random drug tests. Fourth Amendment protections against unreasonable searches by means of involuntary testing are more or less in effect for some, but not all, government jobs. As we noted in Chapter 2, however, these protections do not apply to most private employment situations, where testing for drugs is becoming increasingly popular as the Supreme Court appears to regard the employer's right to know as more important than the worker's right to privacy. The Partnership for a Drug-Free America is actively encouraging private employers to expand drug-testing programs, as is the Office of National Drug Control Policy.

Yes, such programs could be expanded, and, yes, some additional users of illegal drugs could be revealed and there would be some attendant, possibly measurable, reductions in risks to public health and safety; however, it remains proper to doubt the validity of testing as it relates to job performance. A recent review by Lester Grinspoon, a psychiatrist at the Harvard Medical School, asserts that the presence of cannabis metabolites in the urine has no established relationship to drug effects on the brain, and reveals nothing about when or how much of the drug was used or what effect it might have had.[15] Moreover, we should beware of the imperfections in the technology of drug testing: even the best screening tests can yield falsely positive results—with potentially devastating effects on lives and careers. One review reports that radioimmuneassay (RIA) screening of blood may yield false positive rates of 43 percent for cocaine, 42 percent for barbiturates, 21 percent for opiates.[16] Urine tests are also subject to serious false positive results.

Nevertheless, error-borne tragedies aside, suppose we go for broke: the monetary costs of such a program would seem at first relatively small, less than $100 per test. If we are really intent on having a "drug-free society" and one in which anti-drug laws are universally and strictly enforced—leading to a fear-driven reduction in demand—we should find a mind boggling monetary expense: multiply the working population by the cost per test and then multiply the result by, say, three surprise tests annually, and a clearly ridiculous cost picture emerges from an outrageous suggestion.

Aside from the merely stupefying financial costs of such a program, however, the cost in civil liberties, already severe, and the revulsion at the prospect of an ever-expanding police state would, one hopes, make any broad program of coerced ("you don't really have to take the test, but refusing could cost you your job") acceptance of personal prying completely unacceptable.

Education and Propaganda

A more positive approach to demand reduction is education and propaganda in schools, churches, and via newspapers, magazines, radio, and television. Even the staunchest supporters of the criminal orientation to the drug problem agree to this sensible approach to demand reduction. Little is known of the effectiveness of particular educational programs beyond the general finding that the use of marijuana and cocaine among high school seniors seems to have been dropping for the past few years—and even here a causal connection has yet to be established. There is evident opportunity here for improvement in both the quality and quantity of education and propaganda aimed at reducing drug demand. Some of the anti-drug propaganda sponsored by the Partnership for a Drug-Free America, while well-intentioned, is simpy not credible. John Flynn, whose book focuses mainly on cocaine, notes generally that there is near-zero evidence that anti-drug education for young people that is based on fear or on model emulation ("Say No, and you can be like me!") has any useful effect. Flynn argues that only honest and complete information on why people use drugs and what the effects of over-use can be has any chance of being credible and keeping people from tuning out. "Education does not take place when no one is listening."[17] Any policy alternative to the current one of criminalizing the use of certain drugs would have to include a well-planned and patient preparatory program of anti-drug, pro-health education.

Worth noting in this context is the fact that the anti-drug education and propaganda effort of The Partnership for a Drug-Free America focuses on illicit drugs only and says nothing about the hazards of alcohol, nicotine, or prescription drugs—the last being in my town the biggest source of business for the local drug problem hot line. Why is this? The Partnership is supported mainly by grants from pharmaceutically related foundations, the alcohol and tobacco industries, and by the television and advertising industries.[18] Given the level of mutual addiction between these three sets of supporters, it is in no way surprising that the Partnership, whose managers are not motivated to self-destruction, contributes to the national hypocrisy about dangerous drugs. While not intending to minimize the deterrent aspirations behind the Partnership's efforts, I think the risk of implying that nicotine and alcohol are as "American as apple pie" invites further abuse of these drugs, already our most effective killers. Another regrettable aspect of the group's activities is the tendency to exaggerate—or even falsify—for effect. One of their video tapes purports to show the dangerously depressing effect of drugs on brain activity—the wave patterns are essentially flat. A producer of the episode is reported to have later revealed the brain-wave pattern to have been recorded from a person in a coma caused by a wholly extraneous event.

Preventive Intervention

It is reasonable to hope that special programs for young people who are at high risk for becoming drug abusers might reduce those risks if the programs are well conceived and skillfully implemented. Acting on this hope, the Office for Substance Abuse Prevention (OSAP), formerly a part of National Institute on Drug Abuse but now an element of the new Substance Abuse and Mental Health Services Administration, funded 130 demonstration programs beginning in 1987. Eight of the most promising of these projects are described in a 1992 special issue of the *Journal of Community Psychology*.

The editors summarize three main lessons that emerge from the experience thus far:

1. Preventive interventions appear to have their best potential for reducing rates of alcohol and other drug abuse when they are targeted at youth burdened by combinations of risk factors (broken homes, abusive parents, drug user models, arrest records, low income, and poor prospects for fulfilling careers).
2. Developing and implementing a community based intervention is an extraordinarily challenging and complex undertaking. One must not only identify a target population of young people and their families, but design and test procedures for gaining their trust, obtaining and sustaining their participation in the program, securing the (sometimes reluctant) cooperation of existing service agencies.
3. In view of the foregoing, and because of the fairly short duration of the programs, evaluating interventions in terms of impact on alcohol and other drug use rates was extremely difficult; nonetheless, there were signs of modest success on this measure. Investigators were able to take comfort from improvements in other realms of behavior, such as peer and family relations, reductions in proneness to violence, better self-understanding and self-esteem.[19]

My own summary goes like this: Life is complicated for parents and kids that make up high-risk populations, and participation in well-intentioned ameliorative and preventive interventions has to overcome a lot of distractions that are wrought by the poor socio-economic conditions of their neighborhoods. It's hard to get programs established and accepted by families, schools, other neighborhood institutions, and participated in by the youngsters. It is even harder to assess a program's effectiveness because of drop-out rates and other factors over which program leaders have no control. Withall, the effort to develop interventive technology seems worthwhile, and with the accumulation of experience, hope for successful intervention programs is probably justified, especially if—possibly only if—neighborhoods generally improve and their people have reason to expect a safe and satisfying future.

Expanding Opportunities for the Good Life

A final suggestion for reducing drug demand is to discover and implement ways of improving the quality of life of the current and prospective members of the drug abusing population, such that abusers could find better opportunities for personal growth and development and life satisfaction than society now offers. Surely not all drug abuse can be attributed to poverty and its attendant ills—most prominently a hopeless future and a demand for some gratification—but ample research supports the view that for a large number of customers, drugs can provide a quick and easy—though temporary—escape from unpleasant reality.[20] Stanton Peele has persuasively argued that people with something better to do do not do drugs.[21] Proponents of the current policies of staying tough on drugs and crime will see any effort to divert the energies of underprivileged people into work incompatible with drug use as a bleeding-heart effort that would coddle bad people. Badly done, it can be. But carefully planned and consistently applied, a strong public investment in providing opportunities for the underprivileged over a long period of time could go a long way toward reducing the market for the quick and easy escape. This possibility will be discussed at greater length in Chapter 6.

SUMMARY

By no means have the possible actions compatible with the criminalization orientation to the national drug problem been exhausted or even fully tested. Efforts to stop the flow of drugs headed our way from the outside world could be intensified through greater surveillance and interdiction on land, sea, and in the air, or through stronger persuasion of other countries to cut down on the production and exportation of drugs by offers to expand or contract foreign aid. Such actions can be costly not only in dollars but in relations with those countries that are important for reasons beyond our concern for the drug trade. Experience in Colombia and Bolivia shows that there are distinct limits to what we can or should do to cut down the flow of drugs from or through other countries.

Interdicting drugs on our own streets could be expanded—simply by hugely expanding police services. Experience so far shows that shutting down trading in one area is followed by its popping up in another. Truly universal high-density patrolling might be effective, but it would be unacceptably expensive. The additional arrests would surely add to the already heavy cost in crowded court dockets and a demand for still more prison space, which is already the major reason for municipal tax increases.

Random searches and seizures in areas suspected of including drugs, such as subways, buses, markets, and parks, could probably intercept some drugs en route to customers, but the cost in privacy of the many non-transporters of drugs might become intolerably high.

Finally, it would be theoretically possible but politically unacceptable to make alternative careers for practicing dealers sufficiently attractive, through education and job support programs, that users would be hard put to find sellers.

Demand for illegal drugs could be attacked in several ways. Voluntary treatment to eliminate drug habits could be materially expanded, but the lack of convincing data on the effectiveness of drug treatment–programs in relation to their costs lowers the attractiveness of a massive expansion of this alternative.

Involuntary treatment of prisoners and probationers has also been tried. Because the desire to change and the prospect of returning to an environment that would encourage abstinence is largely absent from prison populations and those under court jurisdiction, this road to demand reduction also looks unfeasible.

Random and involuntary urine or other testing for illegal drug use is favored by some, but to do this on a broad enough scale to bring about a significant reduction in drug use would be hugely expensive and extremely offensive to Americans' sense of fairness and their demand for personal privacy.

Anti-drug education and propaganda are favored by the advocates of the criminal orientation to the drug problem as well as by those preferring alternatives. The contents might differ with orientations, but expansion and improvement of the quality and credibility of current efforts would seem a worthy public investment. Development of improved methods of community-based interventions on behalf of high-risk young people should also be pursued.

Finally, to reduce demand by making available more attractive alternatives in life that could, in turn, lower the demand for drugs by members of the underclass is compatible with the criminalization orientation, but of unknown probability of success even if it could overcome the financial and political obstacles confronting it.

In conclusion, it appears that the options, whether practical or wildly impractical, for significantly reducing either the supply or demand for drugs under the current criminalization policies offer little if any prospect of further success. By most measures of public welfare, not only is the current war on drugs failing to solve the problem, but the chances for success coming from just doing more and more of the same thing under the same rules are headed for a solid brick wall at the end of the tunnel.

Chapter 5

What Choices Do We Have?

It is increasingly clear that with our drug problem we have a mess on our hands. People want to have the country freed of the crime and misery that come with illegal drugs, but there is little agreement on how to proceed. There are many possible ways of dealing with the problem, as earlier chapters have suggested, but for each of them there is both a set of ardent and vocal supporters and a set of opponents, with each side of every proposal thinking the other is short-sighted, moralistic, immoral, uninformed, fragmented, too sweeping, judgmental, hasty, rigid, permissive, just plain stupid, or in many other ways flawed. And that is part of the mess—reasonable polylogue is very difficult.

The main reason for this inability to work out the problem, I believe, is the rigid moralistic-legalistic stand of federal policy as expressed by the Office of National Drug Control Policy, particularly as stated in the 1989 edition of the *National Drug Control Strategy*, whose opening paragraph states, "We declare clearly and emphatically that there is no such thing as innocent drug use." That document and its 1992 successor version are described in Chapter 1. To the extent that the general public holds to these views of the far-right components of the second drug culture as described in Chapter 1, one can foresee difficulty in bringing about major policy change.

In what follows, I present a summary of the most prominent current proposals for handling the drug problem, with commentary on each. In the next chapter, I will propose what I think would be the most reasonable policy approach, taking into account what we know of the problem in its many facets and the record of successes and failures thus far. In the final chapter, I will examine the tactics and the legal context of change.

CONTINUING THE DRUG WAR IN ITS PRESENT FORM

To summarize some of the costs that are detailed in Chapter 2: According to the best figures available, the United States in 1985 was spending more than $22 billion in appropriated public funds, and spending more than $2.1 billion in private money defending accused offenders and replacing property destroyed in drug raids or stolen by drug users to support their habits. Additionally, the national economy suffered from lost productivity and lost tax revenues resulting from people being sick, jailed, too soon dead, and from crime victims also being unproductive. These losses came to about $28 billion. Updating these figures to 1988 revealed a total cost to society of more than $58.2 billion. Money costs above this figure come from additional federal government efforts in foreign aid, interdiction, and other activities that add another billion or so to reach a total of well over $60 billion.

These "mere" dollar costs omit the non-monetizeable costs of deteriorating neighborhoods, overcrowded courts and infringements of civil liberties. Also absent from the estimate of total costs are the effects on the economies and political institutions of countries such as Bolivia and Colombia, as they are persuaded to take part in our war on drugs.

On the positive side, the war seems to be producing slow but steady declines in uses of cocaine, marijuana, and heroin, and making people more aware of drug risks and shaping anti-drug attitudes. I emphasize *seems* because, as noted earlier, the data from these changes suffer from serious sampling problems by omitting high school drop-outs and homeless people. Pursuit of the war in its present form over a period of, say, thirty years might continue these desirable trends. Unfortunately, there is no reason to believe that it would not continue most of its harmful byproducts as well: the annual running costs in crime; the prosecution, incarceration, and the non-monetizeable costs of deteriorating neighborhoods; and crowded courts, among others. The rest of the domestic social problems and international relations problems would gradually increase, and the opportunities to use the public and private monies for additional prevention and treatment and for other programs of human development would be forever lost. I think that we have seen enough of the "drug war" approach to conclude that something different is worth trying.

RELAXING CONTROLS ON LEGAL PAIN RELIEVERS

A number of physicians have found themselves in trouble with the law for allegedly overprescribing synthetic narcotics for the relief of pain caused by organic illnesses. Prescription records can raise the suggestion that a physician is supporting an illegal or addictive use of such drugs as Darvon when in fact the physician is concerned only with the control of pain arising from arthritis, degenerative joint disease, various kinds of trauma, or migraine. Regrettably, the specter of "addiction," and of the "addict" as some kind of reprehensible or even dangerous person is associated with the tendency of most physicians to use potentially beneficial narcotics more sparingly than necessary. People tend to forget that drug dependency, a term far preferable to addiction, can be constructively managed by a skilled physician with next to no risk of the patient becoming a danger to herself or others.

After reviewing the literature on drug dependency arising from the treatment of organically based pain, Arnold Trebach concludes that there is no evidence that overprescribing of pain relieving narcotics by physicians has been a major cause of increases in the number drug addicts.[1] He cites a *New England Journal of Medicine* editorial that concludes that the incidence of addiction among patients who receive narcotics is probably no more than one tenth of one percent.

In the same book, Trebach summarizes the case of Dr. Harvey Rose, a board-certified family practitioner in Carmichael, California. It seems that a small proportion of Dr. Rose's patients included some who experienced severe pain arising from various organic causes, and that the prescription records for a still smaller proportion of these had come to the attention of California's Board of Medical Quality Assurance (BMQA), the agency that polices the practice of medicine in the state. After an extensive investigation, including a series of hearings with supporting testimony from the patients for whom Dr. Rose was charged with prescribing excessive amounts of narcotics, BMQA in September of 1982 found against Dr. Rose. The judgment declared that he was guilty of unprofessional conduct, gross negligence, and incompetence because of his prescribing practices, while conceding that none of the violations was motivated by personal gain or profit. The board placed Dr. Rose on seven years of probation and imposed restrictions on how he could prescribe medications. It was only after an extensive battle through the courts and in the media, and with the support of his patients—who had originally been suspected of being drug addicts—that the Sacramento County Superior Court threw the case out on a technicality. Later, after

BMQA threatened to renew the same, plus additional, charges, a compromise was worked out in which BMQA agreed to drop the charges and Dr. Rose consented to take an examination on drug-prescribing practices and be monitored for up to three years by a three-physician panel.[2]

As a result of this case, a new California law was enacted that provided a non-disciplinary but educational approach to physicians found by the Board of Medical Quality Assurance to be misprescribing. A sad commentary on the fear that the idea of "drug addiction" inspires in the medical profession is represented in the reply given by a prominent California physician to the question from Dr. Rose: "What do you do with chronic pain sufferers?" Answer: "I get rid of them."

In Britain, the situation is quite different. Chronic pain sufferers are the beneficiaries of a humane policy that grew from a report by the Rolleston Committee in 1926. Its essence, as summarized by Arnold Trebach, is this: "When a patient is suffering pain from a recognized organic illness, the use of a narcotic drug over a long period of time is presumed to be proper, even though the patient might already be an addict or might become addicted. If the patient is functioning well and living a relatively decent life, the dosage and type of narcotic is considered a private matter between doctor and patient, not at all the business of medical societies or the police."[3] We could do well in this country to educate and legislate our medical practitioners toward such a humane code. This step would by no means "solve the drug problem," but it would do two important things: (1) it would make a significant and visible move toward more humane care of people suffering otherwise intractable pain; and (2) it would document experience that could reduce the public's fear of narcotics and other presently illicit drugs. In other words, it could advance the process of public education so critically important in attaining a drug war–free society.

MEDICALIZATION OF ILLICIT DRUGS HAVING THERAPEUTIC VALUE

Marijuana has long been known to be useful in the treatment of glaucoma, an affliction of the eye characterized by increased pressure of the fluids within and that can lead to blindness, often rather rapidly. It is tetra-hydrocannabinol, THC for short, that is the active ingredient of the marijuana plant that produces the user's recreational high as well as this desired therapeutic effect in a large proportion of glaucoma sufferers whether used alone or in combination with other preparations, such as timolol maleate or pilocarpine. It may be ingested through smoking or pills; smoking seems generally to produce the strongest and fastest beneficial effects. THC has been shown to reduce the nauseating effects of several forms of chemotherapy treatment of cancer patients; one cannabinoid derivative, nabilone, has been approved for treating these effects and classified as a Schedule II drug.

A review of the literature on marijuana effects by Lester Grinspoon reports some success in treating melancholia and other mental illnesses with an extract of cannabis, and in helping addicts withdraw from narcotics use. Also, because one of the striking effects of marijuana is an increase in appetite for food, there is some possibility that the drug may be useful in treating anorexia nervosa, a pathological loss of appetite.[4] Because marijuana itself remains a Schedule I drug under the federal Controlled Substances Act, however, it is not available for any medical use by the public.

There is a small exception to this practice: about 35 people have had special permission from federal authorities to use marijuana in the treatment of a very limited number of conditions in a regulated program of "compassionate investigation of new drugs." The program is in abeyance at this writing, but makes an interesting story because of its potential bearing on treatment for AIDS. This unique situation has come about through the efforts of one Robert Randall, a glaucoma sufferer who dogged the federal drug control establishment for permission to have his physician prescribe marijuana in cigarette form as a treatment. Randall had adventitiously discovered the effectiveness of marijuana for his glaucoma after smoking a joint offered by a friend. Randall petitioned the National Institute on Drug Abuse (NIDA) for permission to have marijuana prescribed as a treatment, drawing on the government crop grown for research uses, but to no avail. To assure a steady supply of his newly discovered treatment, he therefore grew marijuana plants on the sundeck of his apartment, and police happened to spot them which led to his arrest on charges of possession.

Aided by the pro bono services of a prominent Washington law firm, Randall was finally acquitted in the District of Columbia Superior Court. On November 24, 1976, Judge James Washington issued his decision. "The evil he sought to prevent, blindness, is greater than (the evil) he performed to accomplish it, growing marijuana in his residence in violation of the District of Columbia code," he said in explanation of his verdict of not guilty.[5]

The anti-nausea and appetite stimulant effects of marijuana have come to the attention of AIDS patients and their therapists. About three hundred applications for "compassionate investigative new drug" (IND) permits have been filed with the Food and Drug Administration, but have not yet been approved. Marijuana remains a Schedule I substance, that is, too dangerous for use as a prescription medicine, in the face of accumulated evidence that the effects of moderate use of marijuana, especially under prescription control, are for the most part harmless. Bills or resolutions supporting the medicinal use of marijuana have been passed in the legislatures of thirty-five states. Unfortunately the relevant programs can't be implemented because the federal government controls the legal supply.

A general Food and Drug Administration ruling permitting a broad use of marijuana for medicinal purposes is definitely in order. Again, while such a step would not "solve the drug problem" itself, it would provide the two benefits noted above in relation to easing the prohibitions on the medical use of heroin: better treatment and accelerated understanding of marijuana.

EXPERIMENTING WITH NON-ENFORCEMENT OF MARIJUANA LAW

There is a growing understanding, though not yet a consensus, that the biological and behavioral effects of smoking marijuana are far less dramatic and risky than commonly believed. The drug-crazed maniacs depicted in the movie *Reefer Madness*, are no longer expected to emanate from a cloud of marijuana smoke. And yet residual fears persist.

Research on marijuana's effects on behavior and health has been promoted extensively by both the National Institute of Mental Health and the National Institute on Drug Abuse. Grinspoon's review of short-term effects of marijuana use contains these conclusions:

1. There is no evidence that marijuana is more likely than alcohol or nicotine to lead to use of narcotics.
2. Marijuana does not incite people to aggression or violent criminal behavior; a user may say things during a high that she would not ordinarily say, but ordinarily will not do things that are foreign to her nature.
3. Marijuana smoking does not stimulate sexual desire or sexual power.
4. Marijuana produces significantly less impairment of automobile driving ability than alcohol, barely more than a placebo administered in a controlled study using a driving simulator.
5. Several studies support the conclusion that marijuana will not by itself lead to a psychosis in a well-integrated stable person.[6]

Recent official belief on long-term effects is summarized in the testimony of Dr. William Pollin, Director of NIDA, before a congressional committee in 1979:

- Effects on the hearts of young male volunteers in experiments were generally benign.
- Smoking of four or more joints weekly decreased vital lung capacity to about the same degree as one pack of cigarettes daily.
- There is no direct clinical evidence linking marijuana smoke to cancer.
- Research results relating to the immune system are wholly ambiguous.
- There is no reliable evidence relating marijuana smoking to brain damage. Research on damage to monkey brains is inconclusive, with no implications for humans.
- The question of lasting psychological effects remains unresolved. Studies of heavy marijuana users in several countries failed to find evidence of impairment.
- On female reproductive processes, research is limited. One study of 26 users who smoked three times weekly had about three times the number of problematic menstrual cycles as non-users. Nothing is known relating marijuana use to birth abnormality.
- Regarding chromosomal damage, some early studies suggested there might be some, but there is still no good evidence that marijuana causes clinically significant chromosomal damage.

Dr. Pollin concluded: "Any attempt to compare the health impact of marijuana with that of alcohol and tobacco at current levels of use is certain to minimize the hazards of marijuana."[7]

If this conclusion does not by itself imply that marijuana should be released from its current status as a Schedule I substance, it should at least suggest the politically impossible notion that alcohol and nicotine should also be made Schedule I drugs. Fantasy aside, however, the relatively benign known effects of smoking marijuana do recommend marijuana as a candidate for experimentation with a new and less restrictive policy.

The Dutch Experience

Let's consider how the Dutch have handled their problem with illegal drugs. Although perhaps ahead of the story, several interesting comparative statistics will focus on some merits of Dutch policy. First, the number of those addicted to various drugs has remained stable over the past ten years at about 15,000, or about one hundredth of one percent of the total population. This is a rate less than half of the U.S. rate of addiction to heroin alone, setting aside other drugs. Second, the average age of addicts has increased steadily over the past fifteen years to about thirty-one, indicating a reduced recruitment of new young users. Third, the prison population rate per 100,000 citizens in Holland is 35; in Britain there are about 94 people imprisoned for each 100,000 of population. In the United States the figure is 426 per 100,000 residents.[8] Clearly we tend to lock up a lot more of our fellow citizens than do the Dutch or the British. When one notes that drug offenses of all kinds account for at least 10 percent of all imprisonments, one can calculate that about 43 per 100,000 of our fellow Americans are in prison for drug offenses, a ratio higher than Holland's for all offenses.

Now these numbers do not rigorously prove that the different drug laws and policies of Holland and the United States account for the differences in crime and incarceration. They do strongly suggest, however, the worthwhileness of looking into the possibility that drug policy differences might contribute to the differences in crime and incarceration rates. In describing the form and operation of Dutch policies in the next several pages, I drew heavily on the writings of Professor Bruce Bullington of Pennsylvania State University and of Dr. Henk Jan van Vliet of Metropolink Consultancy Research, Amsterdam.

The Netherlands has long been a prosperous, stable, and relatively homogeneous democracy, based on a centuries-old tradition of sailing and trading, and governed generally by consensus and compromise among a small group of religious and political elites. It was not, however, immune from the influences of the rapid changes in the decade following the end of World War II, especially in the 1960s with the developing awareness of various "youth movements" in the Western world. By the late sixties, there was concern over the large increase in illegal drug use and the way the criminal justice system was handling it.

An official commission, the Baan Working Party, was created to study the drug problem in 1968, and its report became the basis for the Dutch Opium Act of 1976. An important principle in the Working Party was the "risk-criterion," which asserted that different illegal drugs and their use were not to be considered equally dangerous; their relative risks should be taken into account in legislation and policy making. Thus, the Opium Act of 1976 distinguished drugs bearing unacceptable risks—heroin, cocaine, LSD, amphetamines—from drugs presenting acceptable risks—hashish and marijuana—and authorized a major decrease in penalities for possessing and retail trading in "cannabis products." A major purpose in the distinction was to split up the supplies of "hard" and "soft" drugs, and to protect the soft drug users from involvement in the hard drug scene and consequent relegation to the fringes of society. The act aimed to create an open and manageable risk situation for young people who were experimenting and to cut off the supply of potential drug addicts. Responsibility for formulating and implementing the policy implications of the new law was given jointly to the Ministry of Justice, and the Ministry of Welfare, Health, and Cultural Affairs, with policy direction residing in the latter.

The upshot of this legislation and its ensuing policies is that drug users in Holland are viewed typically not as criminals, but as individuals who have made personal choices even though those choices may prove damaging to their health or well-being. Minimizing, rather than completely eliminating, the harmful effects of drugs is seen as the main responsibility of government; elimination is simply judged not to be feasible. Such minimization is to be sought through programs of education and a range of voluntary treatment programs specially suited to the particular needs of individual users. The range of typical penalties for drug and other offenders is relatively narrow, in keeping with the lower incarceration rates noted earlier. Although Dutch law defines the use of all illicit drugs as criminal offenses, jail terms and fines tend to be modest, especially with marijuana, whose use is classed as a misdemeanor, punishable by a maximum jail term of one month and a fine of 5,000 florins (approximately U.S. $2,700 at this writing). Hard drug possession can bring a year in jail and a fine of 10,000 florins. Thus, although the penalties normally imposed are gentle indeed by other countries' standards, The Netherlands remains in compliance with the 1961 Single Convention agreements, which require all signatory powers to maintain a criminal status for the sale and use of illicit substances.

Trafficking in illicit drugs is another story, however. The law allows sentences to be longer for trafficking—that is, dealing in large quantities of drugs as opposed to selling small amounts to users—and indeed that is true, with maximum sentences up to twelve years.

How do the law and the actual uses of drugs intertwine? Cannabis products—hashish and marijuana—are readily available in small amounts sold through coffee shops, of which there are about 100 in the city of Amsterdam, 500 country-wide. And under the "expediency principle," which restrains prosecutors from starting criminal proceedings in arbitrarily uniform ways, the possession of 30 grams of cannabis products was placed at the lowest priority level: no prosecution should be undertaken. Prosecutions are the responsibility of the Ministry of Justice, and in practice each of the nineteen judicial districts of the country administers the law according to conditions at the local level. Dealers who appear to sell excessive amounts of cannabis products or promote their sales in ways considered too provoking may be prosecuted, but only after the local authorities, principally the mayor, the chief of police, and the chief public prosecutor agree.

Yet another humane aspect of the Dutch drug policy is the availability, with impunity, of treatment regardless of income for users wishing to change their ways. This applies to users of all drugs. Beyond sustaining a high level of treatment, an important outcome of this aspect of policy is that users can readily be identified and encouraged to seek treatment. Thus, treatment representatives have established contact with about 70 percent of all problem (that is, addicted) drug users. In the United States, because of the high risk of arrest, the comparable figure is estimated at 15 percent. An additional part of the policy is aimed at controlling the spread of disease, especially AIDS, by making readily available hypodermic needles for people addicted to hard drugs, particularly heroin. Needles can be had for free, but only on an exchange basis, an approach specifically designed to keep used needles from being discarded and possibly used again. This aggressive public health orientation has led to a very low incidence of AIDS, hepatitis-B, and other afflictions commonly connected with addiction.

How well has the Dutch policy worked? The policy has been in effect for nearly fifteen years, too short a time for any final assessment; however, a few things seem to be showing up clearly. Users of illicit drugs are not being driven underground or to the fringes of society by a criminalizing orientation to drug use. They are accessible for treatment. Holland has a very low rate of AIDS infection: about 12 percent of all addicts and 25 percent of high-risk intravenous users have tested positive with HIV in Amsterdam, compared with over 50 percent of addicts in the United States. Of the 884 recorded AIDS victims in The Netherlands in 1989, only 80, less than 10 percent, were narcotics addicts, whereas in New York City about 50 percent of AIDS victims were drug addicts.

Predatory crime seems to provide a much smaller proportion of drug users' income in The Netherlands than in the United States: about 22 percent, according to one study. Nearly 28 percent of their support came from public welfare payments, with the balance coming from regular jobs, small-scale drug sales, prostitution, or odd jobs.

Is the Dutch experience transferable to the United States? Probably not rapidly and certainly not on a large scale. Holland enjoys a compact, closely communicating, and relatively homogeneous population. Even if it were politically feasible in the United States (which it is not because of our deeply entrenched view of drug use as a criminal act), the dispersed and heterogeneous population in this country would make it risky to move quickly toward a national policy similar to that of the Dutch. At the very least, however, I believe it would be useful to explore through simulation and other rational means the possibility of emulating the Dutch model on a small scale in one or more accepting communities, possibly in one of the states in which marijuana has already been decriminalized.

The American Experiments

Yes, during the 1970s, eleven states enacted laws removing marijuana from the list of drugs whose possession in small quantities was a felony and reduced the offense to the status of a misdemeanor or minor infraction, and treated it more like a parking ticket than an automobile theft. Those states are Alaska, California, Colorado, Maine, Minnesota, Mississippi, Nebraska, North Carolina, Ohio, Oregon, and South Dakota. Alaska has since abandoned its decriminalization and reverted to the earlier position. (We can watch with interest the outcome of a suit recently filed in Alaska, charging that the rescission of the decriminalization was procedurally improper and in violation of Alaska's constitutional guarantee of a right of privacy.)

What have we learned from the experience in these states? A recent summary of several studies has been prepared by Eric Single of the Canadian Centre on Substance Abuse. The absence of clear data and variations in the laws among the states preclude a general evaluation of the experience. Fortunately, however, in two states before-and-after measures were taken. In Ohio, whose decriminalization law was effective in November 1975, use increased from 27 percent in 1974 to 33 percent in 1978 among people in the 18-to-24 age range. Use increased from 6 percent to 19 percent for people age 25-to-34 over the same period. The proportion of adults in California reporting that they had ever used marijuana increased from 28 percent in February 1975 to 35 percent in November 1976. Depending on one's bias, these data can be interpreted either way, though their authors call the increases in use "modest," a description probably made accurate by an increased willingness to report marijuana use in the absence of the risk of being charged with a felony.

Studies comparing communities or states with and without decriminalization ordinances failed to show differences in marijuana use rates that could be attributed to the change in law. Not surprisingly, data on arrest rates from several decriminalizing states show major declines, and parallel drops in law enforcement costs; also incarceration costs dropped significantly, and income from fines rose.

Single concludes his report:

> Although it cannot be claimed that "decriminalization" has eliminated the social costs and adverse individual consequences associated with marijuana prohibition, it would appear that "decriminalization" has succeeded in reducing the costs without increasing the health and safety hazards associated with use.[9]

A recent indication that Maine's experience with decriminalized marijuana has not been bad comes from the small community of Starks, where the Town Meeting approved, by a narrow margin, a resolution calling for the legalization of marijuana. The resolution called on the legislature to prohibit bans on the cultivation, possession, and sale of cannabis for agricultural and commercial uses, and to legalize possession of as much as two pounds of dried flowering tops for personal use. Similar resolutions have been rejected by three other towns in Maine. Annoyance by helicopter surveillance of possible marijuana plantings may have contributed to the success of the resolution.

Another potentially useful drug that is still held in Schedule I (allegedly high addiction potential and having no known medicinal use) is ibogaine, a hallucinogen derived from a West African plant, Taberanthe iboga. Ibogaine appears to interrupt the biochemical processes that produce the addictive craving for heroin, the heroin substitute, methadone, and other drugs. Recent studies suggest that it is non-addictive, and clinical trials in The Netherlands support claims that ibogaine interrupts for varying periods of time addictions to heroin, cocaine, nicotine, and alcohol. Rigorous trials of the drug have yet to be conducted in the United States. Fortunately, the National Institute on Drug Abuse has agreed to accelerate studies of ibogaine's safety and biochemistry preliminary to approving extensive clinical trials.

CHANGING FROM THE CRIMINAL TO THE PUBLIC HEALTH ORIENTATION

One of the paradoxes of American society is our willingness to help people stricken by misfortune while at the same time being willing to scorn or punish people who dare to differ from accepted folkways. We gladly send our contributions to pay for a child's kidney transplant or to relieve the suffering of people who have lost their homes to fire or flood. And yet we are often quick to blame people afflicted with sexually transmitted diseases or, even today, with alcoholism, saying "it is a problem of their own making." The ethic of individual responsibility remains strong, especially when we are claiming credit for good deeds, or placing blame for bad ones.

In the field of health, however, we have come a long way toward recognizing that many afflictions are not exclusively of our own making, but are the results of complicated interactions of parts of society: communicable diseases, such as measles or poliomyelitis or tuberculosis, were problems because people lived and worked together. People should not be blamed for coming down with them. And with the sexual revolution of recent decades, people are becoming less prone to blame the victim and more willing to see public money spent on prevention or treatment of sexually transmitted diseases. Such afflictions are seen as general problems of people living together in a complex society. They are also recognizable as the source of many costs borne by the public at large, and therefore worthy targets of investments aimed not only at relieving suffering, but at increasing the efficiency of the economy. And finally "they could happen to me or someone in my family."

Alcoholism is now pretty widely accepted—and aggressively promoted by the health insurance and treatment industries—as a "disease" and not just a reprehensible habit. Treatment through self-help groups like Alcoholics Anonymous or in publicly supported hospitals is not only accepted but encouraged—in the interest of relieving both the torment of the alcoholic and the cost in life and efficiency in the society at large.

The essence of public health services is to promote and preserve health and to correct departures from health that impair the well-being and working of the community. Public health workers seek to improve health and reduce illness through whatever legal means are available; they do not seek to place blame on the afflicted, but rather to understand and take steps to remove the causes of the affliction and provide treatment.

Back to our concern with drugs: a good case can be made for seeing drug abuse, or even occasional and casual use that might lead to chronic abuse, as a behavior pattern that arises from the conditions surrounding the user and that too often becomes an addiction or a physiological dependency. Such use and dependency can be seen as a public health problem, whose relief can improve the well-being and working of the community, rather than a criminal behavior that is inherently evil and subject to punishment, or even as a "disease" that has somehow come upon the person, requiring her or him to become a client of the medical system.

A useful distinction can be made between the criminal and public health orientations. There are four general arguments in support of criminal sanctions:

1. They deter bad behavior through the fear of punishment.
2. They can prevent bad behavior by locking the offender away from opportunities to do bad things.
3. They provide society with an opportunity to reform the offender through parole programs or rehabilitation efforts in prisons.
4. They wreak socially acceptable vengeance on wrongdoers.

All four of these reasons apply in our current policies and practices for coping with illicit drugs. None would apply in a pure public health orientation toward such drugs. While continuing to oppose the use of drugs as undesirable, unhealthy, and socially costly behavior, the public health approach would emphasize discovery and alleviation of causal conditions, preventive efforts through education and propaganda (as it now does in efforts to reduce nicotine addiction and alcoholism), and accessible low-cost voluntary treatment at the level of the individual user. But make no mistake about a public health approach being soft on crime: assault, robbery, theft, vandalism, driving under the influence of drugs, and other offenses that are the consequences of—not the acts of—using alcohol or any other drug would remain on the books and punishable under existing codes.

The example of the way the Dutch handle their problem of marijuana use affords a good model of a public health approach, still within the conventional framework of all drugs being illegal. How well the approach might work with the harder drugs of heroin and cocaine is much more open to speculation. In the next chapter, these problems will be analyzed further as we attempt to spell out a broader policy to deal with the national drug problem. We will also spell out other aspects of a policy containing a strong component of public health thinking.

REDUCING PENALTIES FOR DRUG POSSESSION AND USE

Now we move to the more explicit consideration of the arguments for and against decriminalizing and the further step of legalizing currently illicit psychotropic drugs. The two are not the same, either in concept or consequences, but are easily confused.

Decriminalization typically refers to lowering the grade of a law violation from, for example, a felony to a misdeameanor or just to a simple offense, and reducing accordingly the punishments for convicted violators. The law remains on the books, and the proscribed action is still illegal, but it is not judged to be as seriously offensive to society as before. Convicted offenders may become misdemeanants rather than criminals, and so are less stigmatized in the minds of important others—employers, insurers, lenders, police, friends, and neighbors.

Another action similar to decriminalization is a cutback in enforcement: the law and prescribed sentences for violators remain the same, but the police and courts simply do not look for offenses so aggressively. This is de facto decriminalization, and it can be effected on the initiative of the courts and police. Greater flexibility in dealing with local conditions can also be realized.

Legalization implies that acts once forbidden by law are no longer illegal and can be performed without fear of arrest or punishment. It is a far greater liberalization of a once proscribed behavior, and bringing it about would require legislative action to erase prohibition laws from the books. In reference to currently illegal drugs, precipitate legalization, that is, without years of preparation, could present a serious public health risk arising from fast growth in use and abuse, even though it would mean the end of the black market and the crime and other costs of prohibition. Some advocates of reform, such as Mark Kleiman prefer decriminalization to legalization because existing laws, relaxed under decriminalization, could be easily "turned back on" if the decriminalization shows signs of going bad.[10] Moreover, new laws could well turn out to be more stringent and damaging than the older ones.

There is a very large literature on the subject of legalization. The three richest recent reviews are in the special edition of the *Hofstra Law Review* (Spring 1990), a 1991 book by Richard Miller, *The Case for Legalizing Drugs*, and a 1991 set of papers edited by James Inciardi, *The Drug Legalization Debate*. The proceedings of the November 1991 fifth conference on drug policy sponsored by the Drug Policy Foundation contain a wealth of information on practically every aspect of the national drug problem including the legalization issue, nearly all in the cause of various forms of legalization.[11] Because of the extent of the literature, I will only summarize with minimal comment the arguments that have been advanced for and against legalization. Most of the arguments would apply to decriminalization as well. For the reader wishing to dig further into the subject, other useful sources may be found in the references cited for this chapter.

THE CASE FOR CONTINUED PROHIBITION

Legalization, with its attendant lowered prices and eased access, would lead to increased drug use and abuse and their associated costs; the great costs in health and property damage resulting from misuse of alcohol argue against legalizing additional harmful drugs. This is very possibly true, especially if legalization were to happen without extensive advance preparation through education and propaganda.[12] However, experience with marijuana decriminalization thus far suggests that the effect might be temporary and might yield to public education similar to that which has successfully reduced the consumption of nicotine.

Concerning ease of access, most illicit drugs are easily available to anyone willing to risk arrest and at prices most can afford to pay. Richard Miller has summarized a series of surveys that indicate a rather small chance that most of the public would respond with higher drug use—or any drug use—were drugs to be legally available. As Miller says, "The law does not restrain people from destroying themselves; intelligence does. There is no reason to anticipate an epidemic of stupidity sweeping the land if illicit drugs are legalized."[13]

It is possible that advertising of drugs in a legalized market could be regulated, as well it should be, even more strictly than in the present cases for nicotine and alcohol. Peter Hirsch[14] argues that the Supreme Court case known as Posadas *v.* Touring Company[15] supports this prospect. The Court upheld a Puerto Rico law that permitted a set of regulations that had the effect of prohibiting the advertising of casino gambling to local Puerto Ricans but not to tourists. The Court thus held that Puerto Rico had sufficient state interest in trying to control undesirable effects of casino gambling. Whether this precedent could apply to a law specifically directed at the advertising of legalized drugs is highly speculative at this time.

Legalization would send a tacit message that the government approves the use of harmful drugs. Some might think so, but the legalized status of nicotine and alcohol and all the other psychoactive drugs available on prescription does not send that message. The message is: these drugs are not prohibited, and you have to make your own decision about using them.

Prohibition represents the obligation of the majority to protect a minority of citizens from evil. This view has some appeal, drawing as it does on a communitarian ethic; however, the people for whom protection is supposedly provided usually have no say in whether they desire that protection, and the argument turns out to be essentially a paternalistic one that says "Father (read: established law enforcement and political elite) knows best." Truly beneficent paternalism requires a level of love and understanding that is absent from the criminal orientation toward potential drug users.

Increased use would, through increased illness, produce a loss of human capital to U.S. market competitiveness. People who are sick for whatever reason become a drag on the economy. The counter-argument could point to the figures (see Chapter 2) that show incarceration costs and the costs of pursuing criminals instead of legitimate careers are far greater than the economic losses due to illness or early death. Experience in cities where clean needles are legally and cheaply available has shown a marked reduction in needle-transmitted illnesses.[16]

As a kind of regulation, having the government operate stores selling seemingly bad things is hypocritical. This argument is valid against the state liquor store system still extant in a few states. The argument has merit, and the state store is only one way, possibly a very good way, to regulate sales of potentially harmful recreational drugs. But unless it were to be adopted nation-wide, a very unlikely prospect, that form of regulation would not spread the hypocritical message very far.

Legalization would offer permissiveness for further self gratification. True. Gratification of the self is a basic human need that is manifested in every society and walk of life, and should be. Puritanical opposition to having fun in the short run without having paid for it through deserving work is part of the drug problem, even though our folkways and mores—and certainly our advertising and credit card industries—advocate pleasure in the present and payment in the future.

Legalization would pose an impossible preventive and remedial task for anti-drug education. A large task, to be sure, and one that is already under way and with some apparent successes. The work should be improved and expanded, even under today's conditions. We can take heart that the educational efforts to persuade various population groups to cut down on smoking and drinking are having measurable effects.

Children, the most vulnerable members of society, would be put at special risk. This is true, and very special efforts would have to be put forth to protect them, through regulation of sales and parent education, better schooling and other opportunities to do things that can compete with drugs as a form of self-gratification and fulfillment.

Finally, it is argued that treaties obligate the United States to maintain a criminalized position for heroin, marijuana, and cocaine. This is not true. Article 46 of The United Nations Single Convention on Narcotic Drugs, adopted in Geneva in 1961 and endorsed by the United States in 1967, provides a loop-hole that allows any signatory power to release itself from the treaty on six months notice.

THE CASE FOR LEGALIZATION

Before listing the arguments for legalization, I want to point out that there is less than unanimity on what legalization means, much less on how to bring it about. To illustrate the complexity of the idea, here are a few proposals:

- full legalization, with over-the-counter purchases like candy or Gas-X;
- legalization with sales strictly controlled by sale through government stores;
- legalization except for minors, as in the present case of alcohol in most places;
- legalization under strict medical prescription, as is currently the case with other drugs having potentially dangerous side effects;
- legalization under loose medical prescription, as when the friendly family physician okays a sleeping pill virtually on request;
- legalization under the supervision of government-controlled clinics, similar to the way methadone has been dispensed, but with full voluntarism; and
- decriminalization, as has been done for marijuana in Holland and several American states already.

One can easily imagine variations within these variations. But here are the main arguments that have been put forth for legalization:

- With reductions in drug prices the black market will disappear, criminal careers will become less attractive, and drug-associated crime will be reduced, leading to safer streets and homes.
- Prison overcrowding along with the often terrible consequences for prisoners would be relieved ("I was sentenced to confinement, not to rape").
- Prisons could retain dangerous inmates serving sentences for violent crimes rather than granting them early release or parole in order to make room for drug offenders.
- Police resources would be released for more urgent duties than arresting street-level dealers and users.
- Municipal courts would be relieved of clogging by the hundreds of daily cases of drug charges now being processed.
- Corruption of officials now connected with the drug laws would be eliminated, along with the cynicism about the law that corruption breeds.
- Tax money now going into law enforcement would be saved or released for more urgent and constructive uses.
- The erosion of personal liberties, via search-and-seizure in over-zealous drug busts and intrusive urine testing would be slowed or stopped. This is not to say

that checks should not be made for the *effects* of drug use on job performance, especially in jobs whose performance affects public health and safety—bus drivers, airline pilots, surgeons, for example. But such checks are not the same as urine or saliva tests, which show whether or not someone has ingested a drug sometime in the past. Performance is what we should be interested in, not whether someone has chosen to drink alcohol or smoke a marijuana cigarette a day or two ago.

- Several foreign governments would be relieved of the de-stabilizing forces generated by U.S. insistence on cooperation in our war on drugs. To recur to a single example, DEA officers in Turkey assured me that their intelligence data shows clearly that the disruptive activities of the Workers Party of Kurdistan, or PKK, which is a terrorist organization based in Lebanon, are significantly financed by proceeds from the international drug trade. There is a fairly extensive literature on the extent to which various insurgencies—whether of the political right or left—have been financed through the trade in illegal drugs.[17]

SUMMARY AND CONCLUSION

There may be light at the end of the long tunnel through the drug problem, and our task is to select the most effective way to get to it. We have reviewed a number of possibilities in this chapter, in preparation for a plan that, in my opinion, has a reasonable chance for success.

We can continue the drug war in its present form. Despite some apparent successes in reducing actual drug use and in making the public less interested in using drugs, the war seems to be costing more in many ways than we are getting from it. It is time to try something different.

Relaxing controls on pain-relieving drugs would provide a modest start by making relief from intractable pain more readily available and by offering the possibility of demonstrating that some good can come from change.

Similarly humane treatment and useful knowledge could derive from extending cannabis use in areas where it has proven to have therapeutic value.

We can experiment further with non-enforcement of marijuana laws, emulating and building on the Dutch experience, and taking advantage of the record accumulated thus far in the several American states that have decriminalized marijuana.

A broader view of drug use as a public health issue rather than a crime problem is surely worth examining closely.

What is clear from all this is that there is no neat or simple way to do away with the war-on-drugs metaphor. Drug law reform can only come slowly and after extended public discussion and analysis and comparison of the many variations on decriminalization or legalization. In the next chapter, I will present a new policy proposal and its philosophical rationale. The final chapter will address the legal context for a policy change and the steps for getting there from here.

Chapter 6

Toward a New Policy

Now comes the hard part: What should a new national drug policy be, and how can it be brought about? The broadest outline for goals is easy: like any public policy, a new national policy on drugs should promise more good than harm, and the costs of making a change to the new should be more than offset by reductions in the cost of continuing the old. The outline for tactics in bringing about change is less clear, for change always involves risks to a range of attitudes, values, and convictions deeply rooted in various parts of the society. Change also threatens interests that are firmly vested in the processes that create and the institutions that implement and protect the current policy. Analysis of the goals and presentation of a new policy is the task of this chapter. The final chapter examines conditions and tactics for change.

As a reminder of today's situation and of the difficulty of effecting reform, it is interesting to note what Edward Brecher wrote more than twenty years ago in what is yet the most comprehensive review of America's drug problem. Focusing on heroin, Brecher wrote:

> Many American morphine and heroin addicts prior to 1914 led long, healthy, respectable, productive lives despite addiction—and so do a few addicts today. The sorry plight of most heroin addicts in the United States today results primarily from the high price of heroin, the contamination and adulteration of heroin available in the black market, the mainlining of the drug instead of safer modes of use, the laws against heroin and the ways in which they are enforced, the imprisonment of addicts, society's attitude toward addicts, and other nonphar-

macological factors. It was the enforcement of the Harrison Act of 1914 that converted opiate addiction from what it had long been—a misfortune and a disgrace—into a disaster.[1]

Before going ahead, I offer this reminder: reducing the controls on currently illegal drugs, including especially the extreme of full legalization and the elimination of virtually all controls, will not by itself eliminate or even materially reduce the drug-use problem. What can be expected is a reduction in many of the costs connected with the problem, especially those generated by the "war on drugs"—crime, prosecution, incarceration, interdiction, crime-related neighborhoods and family deterioration, a faltering criminal justice system, infringements of civil liberties, and corruption and militarization of democratic governments in drug-supplying countries, to mention a few.

About policy goals, my contention is, and my argument will be, that the risks of increased drug use resulting from a relaxation of controls, serious as those risks might be, can themselves be controlled; and, further, that the relief from the encumbrances of the war on drugs can with astute management more than compensate society for the risks of greater drug use.

About policy tactics, my contention is that the American citizenry can be brought to see that the values underlying a more liberalized policy on currently illicit drugs are fundamentally harmonious with basic attitudes toward individual liberty, justice, and personal responsibility; these values are antagonistic to a policy that justifies a "big brother" state that deprives people of their freedoms more than it protects them from the wrongdoing of fellow citizens. Specific tactical options are taken up in the next chapter.

I believe that a fairly straightforward comparison of the evident economic costs and benefits of old versus new policies will be persuasive only for some people and not at all for others. People who believe fundamentally that "drugs are inherently and always bad" or that "pleasure should always and only be earned through hard work" or that "people who use illegal drugs are weak in character and unworthy of respect" will be unmoved by arguments about economic or social efficiency. Benefit/cost comparisons do not work in the abortion argument: no matter how thoroughly those whose views are "pro-choice" might show the benefits to society of having fewer unwanted children—potentially sick, abused, abandoned, unemployed, or criminal—those with opposing views (the so-called "pro-lifers") can say with unalterable commitment that every human life is, and should always be, without price of any kind. I will therefore rely on both the economic (and quasi-economic) arguments and the arguments of human rights and liberties in trying to make my case.

DRUG POLICY GOALS

Looking back to Chapter 2, where many of the costs of the drug problem were summarized, and to Chapter 3, where the criteria for judging the effectiveness of present policy were set forth, let us relate those criteria and some of the cost factors more specifically to what the goals of a national drug policy should be.

Reducing Physical and Mental Health Risks

Hazards to the physical and mental health of potential drug users and their family members should be minimized. Present laws and regulations governing the prescription and use of pharmaceutical drugs work reasonably well in protecting the physical health of people requiring such drugs. True, there are abuses with and without the cooperation of physicians empowered to prescribe them; there are diversions of prescription opiates into the black market and occasional robberies of pharmacies; and there are still needless restrictions on the access that afflicted people have to pain-relieving drugs. But on the whole, the system works pretty well. Drugs that are primarily psychoactive in function, such as flurazepam (sleep inducers), diazepam (tranquilizers), or thorazine (to control the mood swings of manic-depressive psychosis) are also subject to abuse through overdependency of the users and too-easy accommodation of users by prescribers. But being in the open market and at the same time generating records of their use, practically all prescription drugs are subject to two kinds of control: (1) quality control, exercised through the oversight of the Food and Drug Administration and by competition in the market; and (2) abuse exposure by means of the prescription-record system.

I believe that a distribution system for currently illicit drugs, specifically cocaine, heroin, and marijuana (and their derivatives) that would make them legally available at market prices and with personal identification and signature records of sale to people at least 18 years of age, would go a long way toward protecting the physical and mental health of those who would use them. Such availability would also undercut the demand for dangerous "designer drugs" that can be formulated more rapidly than the law can detect and illegalize them.

Needles for injecting drugs would be purchasable or available at no cost in exchange for used ones as protection against the risks of infection from contaminated needles. There are ample data[2] to support the claim that the availability of clean needles can reduce the incidence of hepatitis and

AIDS; needle exchange programs are already in effect in Stratford, Connecticut and Washington, D.C. Purity and quality of product would be encouraged through market competition (as allegedly they are for nicotine and alcohol products). Rapid spread of consumption would be discouraged by restrictions on advertising as well as by expanded education and propaganda campaigns specifically designed for particular risk groups. Moreover, the greater reliability of product quality would contribute to reducing the individual user's demand for drugs. Why? Because assured rewards from buying in a legal market would tend to produce less compulsively driven behavior than erratic rewards that come from seeking drugs in the illicit market. The mental health component of this particular policy goal would be advanced in part by eliminating the guilt and fear of arrest that accompanies the violation of law, by removing the stigma that are now stamped on convicted offenders, and reducing the severity of conflict within the home.

Sustaining Neighborhood Quality and Safety

National drug policy should aim to improve the quality of neighborhood life and the safety of the streets. It has been extensively documented that the illegality of both the use and sale of heroin, cocaine, and marijuana has contributed tragically to the decline of neighborhood quality in cities all across the country, and that the decline is due primarily to the illegality of those substances and their attendant black markets and turf wars. A relaxation of controls, along the line suggested just above, would undercut the incentives to criminal sales—even at the risk of depriving many inner-city youth of the most lucrative youth employment program of the century.

Efficient Allocation of Anti-Drug-Use Resources

National drug policy should encourage reasonably efficient allocations of resources particularly designed to alleviate the drug-use problem; it should also seek to reduce costs, monetary and others, that result from the present fact that the sale and use of some drugs are illegal.

The economic data presented in Chapter 2 show (1) that the use problems of both alcohol and the illicit drugs call for huge sums of appropriated tax money to be spent on the "core costs" of treatment and treatment support (mainly research and training); and (2) that they evoke still larger and broadly borne costs in lost productivity of people sick, imprisoned, pursuing criminal careers, or "prematurely" dead. The costs of the alcohol problem far exceed those of the illicit drug problem simply because there are about four times as many alcohol abusers.[3]

Those data also show (see Chapter 2, Table 2.2) that the total direct costs to the criminal justice system of the illicit drug problem are more than three times those of the alcohol problem. A rough calculation of a crime cost per abuser—taken by dividing the total crime cost of alcohol abuse by four—would suggest that the war on drugs causes the drug problem to be about twelve times as costly on an individual basis as the alcohol problem. A look at the indirect costs per abuser in the same way suggests that the war on drugs makes drug users about twenty-four times more costly than users of alcohol—and offers a fine opportunity for cutting costs.

Does this in turn suggest that a reallocation of resources now consumed in the pursuit of criminal drug trading and use to some other aspect of the drug problem might produce significant net public gains? To me it certainly does, with treatment and preventive education (both relatively primitive technologies at present) being among the targets for reallocation. But let not legalization advocates be carried away too soon by this reallocation idea. Although desirable in principle, it is not something that can be done by administrative fiat or legislative action without a lot of struggle. This practical problem will be discussed later in the chapter.

This objective should also seek to effect reductions in costs not easily expressible in dollar terms, especially costs to civil liberties, and here, too, opportunities abound. We must accept the fact that law enforcement systems, like all social systems, are prone to inefficiencies and corruption; a drug policy that makes millions of dollars available for the "purchase" of special favors from police, courts, and prisons invites the extremes. But even if corruption is not taken into account, our courts are suffering from the pressures of an overload of drug-related cases that have at least two negative effects on civil liberties: First, drug law offenders are often being "processed" with plea-bargaining offers that too often result in pleas of guilty to lesser offenses they may have committed so as to avoid risk of being found guilty of more serious offenses with which they are charged; in the "bargain," they are being denied Sixth Amendment rights "to a speedy and public trial by an impartial jury." Second, people charged with other offenses or seeking redress of grievances through civil law are forced to accept otherwise avoidable delays in having their cases heard—who was it that said "justice delayed is justice denied"?

Still other costs in civil liberties were described in Chapter 2—abuse of the "exclusionary rule," denial of Fourth Amendment protections against unreasonable searches and seizures, erosion of Eighth Amendment protections against cruel and unusual punishments. And these make up but a small sample of the extensive literature on this part of the drug problem.

Managing a Tolerable Level of Drug Use

National drug policy should recognize that the management of a tolerable level of drug use can have a number of specific economic and social advantages: (1) reduction in the costs now incurred by the "war on drugs"; (2) additional revenue from an appropriately taxed legal drug trade; and (3) the reallocation of the combined net gains to other human development objectives. I have already reminded us of the number of tax dollars—around sixteen billion of them—that are spent annually in response to drug-related crime and in the effort to control the flow of drugs into the United States. These funds plus the dollars of revenue generated from taxes on drug sales could do many good things aimed principally at preventing drug abuse, plus be put toward additional research on improving treatment and anti-drug education technologies.

It is important to note that prevention of drug abuse is commonly taken to mean education and propaganda aimed toward making people decide against drug use. In my view, education is not the most potent option in the pursuit of prevention. A recounting of the story of American soldiers returning from Vietnam will make the point by drawing on research by Lee Robins and her collaborators.[4]

As the Vietnam War went on, reports of wide-spread abuse of heroin raised fears that returning soldiers would mean increased numbers of addicts roaming the streets. Estimates of addiction rates ran as high as 25 percent, but intensive searching by military authorities turned up a smaller number of "users," not addicts—about 4 percent. According to another study, about half of the troops had tried opiates once, and 20 percent claimed regular use; but there were no reports of adverse effects on combat performance. The soldiers explained that boredom and fear led to the discovery that heroin could ease these pains. In other words, they found relevant reasons in their life situations to turn to drugs.[5]

Interestingly and not surprisingly, when Vietnam soldiers returned to the States, their use of heroin tended to disappear, along with the reasons for that use. About half of those who had been addicted to heroin in Vietnam used heroin on returning home, but only a small fraction of those formerly addicted became re-addicted. What was happening was a set of changes in life settings that made doing other things more rewarding than using drugs. "Drugs do not cause addiction. Addiction is something that users do to themselves,"[6] and "Those with better things to do are protected from addiction."[7] These two quotations from Richard Miller and Stanton Peele, respectively, summarize a large number of studies—of teenage, out-of-school drug users, college student cocaine samplers, and middle-class adult users who discover that drug use is not as rewarding as they once thought it was and that being productively engaged is far more satisfying. Peele summarizes: "Going to college, reading books, and striving to get ahead make it less likely that people will become heavy or addicted drug users or alcoholics. Having a good-paying job and a good social position makes it more likely that people can quit drugs or drinking or cut back when these produce bad effects."[8]

Regarding national drug policy, to me these facts and conclusions argue for the reallocation of present tax dollars from the war on drugs to truly preventive efforts. These efforts should come in the form of better schools generally, more and better training for productive work in shops and factories, improved housing, child care for children of working parents, and child health clinics—in other words, for programs that will promote human development and establish the basis for hope in people making up the population segments at highest risk of seeking gratification or relief through drug and alcohol use.

Given the mediocre performance of the national economy in general, coupled with the capitalist tendency always to widen the gap between the haves and the have-nots, I would also argue that drug war funds could well be assigned to public employment programs. These could be modeled on the Civilian Conservation Corps (CCC) of the 1930s or on today's Volunteers in Service to America (VISTA) and could offer job training and opportunities for a measure of independence and self-respect for people who otherwise would have to rely on more demeaning welfare programs. Two generations of this kind of policy might go a long way toward eliminating role models that teach sloth and dependency, and even help develop an economy that can compete more effectively in world markets.

Improving International Relations and Encouraging Democracy

National drug policy should aim to reduce frictions between the United States and other countries, and encourage the development and strengthening of democratic forms of government in them. Our official stance has long been in favor of democratizing politics in Latin American countries, even if our actions have often not comported well with it. American drug policy has in recent years had special bearing on Peru, Bolivia, and Colombia, whose economies are at this time heavily dependent on the world drug trade and whose democratic institutions are placed at risk by American insistence on cooperation with the "war on drugs." Mexico, too, has been impacted by our drug war because it provides major routes for the transport of drugs from South America. The hazards to these countries have been extensively documented and were summarized in Chapter 2.

American drug policy options that would affect our Latin American neighbors include the following:

1. Continue efforts to persuade (coerce?) these countries to continue or expand cooperation in our efforts to reduce or eliminate the northward flow of drugs.
2. Expand U.S. military intervention within those countries in an effort to stop the growth of coca, its refinement into cocaine, and the shipment of the ensuing product out of the country.
3. Abandon both of the above, and concentrate on stopping the flow of drugs into the United States and their later distribution within the country. (This option has no chance of being followed short of some degree of drug legalization within the United States.)

The second option has begun to gain favor within parts of the U.S. military after years of resistance, due largely to the decline in the threat posed by world communism and the associated rise in threats to American military budgets and influence. According to a review by Donald Mabry, as recently as 1988, Stephen Olmstead, Assistant Secretary of Defense for Drug Policy and Enforcement, argued that the drug war was not a war but a crusade and further claimed that not all national security threats, such as a weak economy, fell within the purview of the military simply because they might be called national security threats.[9] Former Defense Secretaries Caspar Weinberger and Frank Carlucci argued that military people are not trained as police and should not be so used, that the military mission was to protect the United States from foreign military action, not from drug smugglers. But with the demise of the Soviet empire the official policy changed, and Defense Secretary Richard Cheney made clear to the Defense Department that "illicit trafficking in narcotics and all that goes with it is, indeed, a national security problem." Cheney added, "The supply of illicit drugs to the United States from abroad, the associated violence and international instability, and the use of illegal drugs within the country pose a direct threat to the sovereignty of the country. The threat of illicit drugs strikes at the heart of the nation's values."[10] This is pretty strong language from a position that two years previously had cautioned strongly against U.S. military involvement in the war on drugs. How easy it is to allow official departmental thinking to be captured by a metaphor, and then to use that fact to advocate action long opposed as being contrary to the department's historic mission!

So now the U.S. defense establishment is at risk of being dragged into a "war" that is already being lost[11] and cannot possibly be "won" short of massive direct intervention that would premanently sever the good relations that have been cultivated, albeit erratically, for decades with Latin American governments. Military participation currently being planned under the doctrine of Low Intensity Conflict would have American troops train more and more units of Colombian, Peruvian, and Bolivian armies in tracking down and destroying cocaine processing centers and capturing the leaders of the drug trades in those countries.

According to another study by Mabry, there remain major divisions with the American military establishment over this idea, with the Southern Command, based in the Panama Canal Zone, being the only outfit itching to get involved in the Andes.[12] The risk of gradual escalation into another Vietnam-like quagmire is a source of concern, as is the fear that American forces could follow their Latin American counterparts into the morass of corruption that the drug business so richly offers.

Let it be noted that all of this potential action by the U.S. military is far from welcomed by the governments of Peru, Colombia, and Bolivia. Their own internal political and economic scenery make the prospect of increased power of their military establishments appear ever more threatening to incumbent governments. And the prospect of economic loss to Bolivia's more than 40,000 coca-growing families and Peru's 200,000, plus the opposition from democratically inclined political parties, farmers' syndicates, and labor unions is daunting, to say the least.

Finally, and in anticipation of moral arguments for changing our national drug policy, we can question the morality of abusing our power in our relations with these critical Latin American countries. Is it fair for the United States, which accounts for about 22 percent of Colombia's legal exports, 33 percent of Bolivia's, and 26 percent of Peru's, to insist on the cooperation of those countries in solving America's own drug problem?[13] Should this degree of economic leverage, plus the leverage of foreign aid grants and loans, be used to pressure those countries into risky actions on behalf of our drug war?

In summary, the economic and military clout of the United States in pursuing the solution of the American drug problem in Latin America is already disruptive to established governments and fragile democratic institutions. Legalization of drugs back home could eliminate many of the concerns to our south, and might even give credibility to allegations that we want a "Good Neighbor Policy" (of Franklin Roosevelt) and to form a "Partnership for Progress" (of John Kennedy) with our Latin American neighbors.

Ensuring Civil Liberties and Individual Freedoms

A final, and most important objective of national drug policy should be to enhance the moral quality of relationships between citizens and the organs of government. This broad objective includes the defense of two classes of rights. First are rights generally asserted "to be self-evident, that all men are created equal, that they are endowed by their Creator with certain unalienable rights, that among these are Life, Liberty, and the pursuit of Happiness," and ascribed to persons as a consequence of being human. The terms "human rights" and "natural rights" are frequently mentioned in this context. Second are rights that are formally created through public consensus and established in political documents, especially the Bill of Rights in the U.S. Constitution, plus more specific affirmations in various state constitutions.

This objective also encompasses widely accepted ethical practices—moral principles if you will—that we are constantly enjoined to follow in both public and private transactions: telling the truth, keeping promises, respecting the autonomy and freedom of other people, being fair in our treatment of others, being consistent in the values we apply in making decisions, and avoiding harm to others. These practices are not only good in themselves from the ethicist's viewpoint, but are good and useful in keeping relations between individuals and the machinery of society functioning reasonably well.

A number of writers on drug policy, among them James Ostrowski,[14] Steven Wisotsky,[15] and David Richards[16] have argued the primacy of preserving the freedom of individual choice in what one does to one's own body. I join them in subscribing to a general human rights perspective on what should be the principles limiting the power of the state to intervene in individual lives. Drawing on the thought of John Locke, Jean Jacques Rousseau, and Immanuel Kant, and more recently the work of John Rawls,[17] this perspective emphasizes the central values of autonomy and equality as basic rights that people should enjoy and that the state has the duty to defend. In its essence, this human rights perspective asserts that a contractual relationship exists between the people and their institutions of government, such that each person is to have an equal right to the most extensive basic liberty compatible with similar liberty for others. Holding the primacy of autonomy and equality in the heirarchy of values differs from John Stuart Mill's and Jeremy

Bentham's utilitarian positions, which stress the goodness or badness of the consequences of an act or a policy.[18]

While utilitarian thought is appealing to most Americans, practical as we claim to be, it has a major drawback as the ultimate guide to public policy: it lacks a moral basis for answering the question "Who decides what the good outcomes are that should be promoted by an action or a policy?" When the question is answered by referring to majority rule, members of the minority are instantly at risk of losing more fundamental rights to personal autonomy and equality of standing. The American judicial system is designed to defend rights of minorities according to principles set forth in the Bill of Rights. Nonetheless, the self-aggrandizing nature of humans makes it difficult to the ensure that "practicality," as interpreted by the elected majority and their judicial appointees, will not prevail over the human rights of hundreds of thousands of their fellow citizens.

Because of this shortcoming, utility-based ways of evaluating public policy should be viewed with skepticism, and their desired or forecasted outcomes should be assessed against their effects on individual autonomy and equality of standing. Even though I have argued the economic benefits of calling off the drug war, I continue to question the ultimate virtue of benefit/cost analysis as the basis for final policy decisions: Who selects the benefits and the costs to be compared? Only when they suggest opportunities for increasing and widely ensuring autonomy and a degree of equality consistent with that autonomy should benefit/cost analyses be taken seriously as policy guides.

From the human rights position, one must assert that prohibition violates a moral right to control one's mind and body and advocates the use of physical force to do this. The position is bolstered by the factual argument, well documented by this time that the direct physical effects of using most drugs in the way they are mostly used—that is, occasionally or frequently but not "addictively"—are far less dangerous to the users and to others than dedicated drug warriors would have us believe.[19] This weakens the paternalistic argument that the state through its criminal codes has the right and duty to protect all people against harming themselves or engaging in disgusting consensual acts that inflict little if any harm on others. Ostrowski argues that the consequences of individual rights violations include, in addition to a loss of control over one's life, deprivation of the opportunity of facing and overcoming a challenge, and an associated reduction in human capital as a result of the state's preventing the development of personal problem-solving abilities.

Assigning the status of "disease" to drug use and abuse further detracts from human dignity by turning the solution of one's problem to the medical profession, as Stanton Peele has eloquently argued in *The Diseasing of America*. "Diagnosing" the abuse of alcohol and other drugs as a disease has the convenient legal effect of relieving a person of responsibility for reckless driving, spouse abuse, or other crimes simply because she is "out of control" or "unaware of the act"; being sick is not a crime but is often a convenience. As a single but prominent example, Washington D.C.'s former mayor Marion Barry, when charged with various drug-related offenses, claimed in his defense that he was under the influence of a disease and "out of control." Regrettably, absolving one of responsibility for criminal acts does nothing to strengthen one's capacity for effective life-management, and the absolving "diagnosis" simply passes the task and the opportunity for self-development to a third party.

In the realm of ethical interpersonal relations, we have seen drug warriors encouraging young people to report drug use by their friends, even their parents—all in the name of upholding the law. Steven Wisotsky reports that under Florida's very stiff trafficking law a defendant who offers substantial assistance to the state may be offered a prosecutor's recommendation for a more lenient sentence or even probation if he will name other transgressors of the drug law, thus creating a batch of amateur under cover agents eager to find ways of escaping the worst of the otherwise mandatory sentences.[20]

It is well worth noting that members of the clergy nation-wide are becoming increasingly concerned about the failures of current drug policy and are speaking out "against the immorality of a policy that is systematically destroying families all over the country." While not denying the potentially serious effects of drug abuse, the broadly based interdenominational Religious Coalition for a Moral Drug Policy asserts that many of the dire consequences of the drug war

> spring from the ideological assumption that we must make everything we disapprove of illegal. We reject this notion, as it forgets the difference between vice and crime. Enforcing public morality is our responsibility as individuals, parents and as clergy. To put the government in charge of all morality is to abdicate our individual responsibility, to weaken the moral authority of our religious institutions, and thus to fail in the execution of our duties.[21]

If we are interested in consistency in the basis for making judgments and decisions we should at least take note of the hypocrisy that characterizes current drug policy. Far more lives are ruined by the use of nicotine than by the consumption of illicit drugs: fewer than 7,000 annual deaths are attributable to all illicit drugs, compared to nicotine's annual toll of around 400,000. Yet the purveyors of tobacco products can not only promote their products enthusiastically, but also earn a tax break for doing so, not to mention the farm subsidies that tobacco growers also receive.

According to Richard Miller, the physical dangers of nicotine are so well known that the 1970 drug control law had to exempt nicotine specifically, for it fit the scientific criteria that were used to define drugs that were banned. Most Americans just do not consider alcohol a drug: it is viewed as a normal part of life, even though many people use it badly to their own and other people's detriment. Annual alcohol-related deaths come to about 33,500, not counting the 50,000 deaths from injuries and accidents.[22] We tolerate, even enjoy, several drug-free addictions, such as to food (obesity), to food with vomiting (bulimia), to jogging and other sports, none of which is criminal or vicious, though these "addictions" may fundamentally be cravings as morbid as those for alcohol or heroin. Even Vice President Dan Quayle replied to *Washington Post* reporter Bob Woodward's commenting about Quayle's enthusiasm for golf by saying, "I can't get enough of it!"[23]

My own view on individual rights accords with those I have cited. I agree with Wisotksy and others who assert that the use of all recreational drugs should be looked on as situations of individuals making their own choices in the search for pleasure and fulfillment, and that even though such choices may often have bad consequences, the state should not prohibit them. The state should, however, persist in enforcing the law against illegal consequences of drug use that harm others and limit their freedom, as is now done against offenders under the influence of alcohol.

The civil rights conferred by the first ten amendments to the American Constitution are indeed remarkable in the history of states and their relations to citizens. The freedoms specified in this Bill of Rights are vigorously defended in courts across the land against assaults from many quarters. Some examples have been cited in Chapter 2, which includes the loss of civil liberties among the more serious costs connected with the drug problem and are especially derivative from the drug war. However, the case for the morality objective of drug policy, particularly related to principles of fairness and consistency, may be strengthened by a reminder of additional abuses that a moral policy should eliminate.

Among the oppressive tools available to the drug war effort is civil commitment to a mental hospital, or other treatment program, of a person charged with drug abuse. This is an especially convenient practice for prosecutors who lack sufficient evidence to produce a criminal conviction, for neither the Sixth Amendment right to question accusers and to be defended by a lawyer nor the Eighth Amendment prohibition against cruel and unusual punishment applies in such civil cases. Thus, it is possible to incarcerate, and for an indeterminate period, a person not convicted of any crime—another abuse of individual liberty made possible by labelling drug abuse a "disease." As Miller puts it, "The sham works because drug abuse is a crime with medical symptoms—no one would receive civil commitment for the 'disease' of burglary."[24]

The passion for strict enforcement of anti-drug laws has bred numerous offenses against civil liberties. The Comprehensive Crime Control Act of 1984 authorizes pre-trial detention if a judge finds that a defendant's release on bail would pose a danger to the community and dispenses with pre-trial bail for most charges under the Controlled Substances Act if it is deemed necessary to protect the community from even non-violent crimes like drug trafficking. The injustice occurs by imposing on the accused severe handicaps in preparing an effective defense.

Another incursion into defendants' rights can arise when a prosecutor requests (under the 1984 Crime Control act) that the court order an attorney defending an accused who is in the end convicted to forfeit fees to the United States. One need not feel sympathy for overpaid lawyers to recognize that people accused of drug offenses may find competent representation hard to come by. Steven Wisotsky quotes a prominent defense attorney on retiring from drug cases: "It's just not worth the aggravation to represent major drug dealers. The government comes after your fees. . . . I like to do one murder case a year. It's okay to represent a murderer. Everyone approves of that."[25]

The zeal with which legislators will pursue the image of "being tough on drugs" is revealed in a *New York Times* report summarized by Joan Johnson that the Delaware state senate seriously considered public flogging as a possible punishment for drug pushing, and that the District of Columbia hopes to expand its anti-loitering law, which allows authorities to order people out of an area and arrest people who gather in groups of two or more. Maryland's Congressman Steny Hoyer was quoted as saying, "You have members—good solid members—come through the door and say 'I don't care if it's constitutional; we can leave constitutionality up to the courts'."[26]

Enforcement zeal, promoted by the Drug-Free Schools and Communities Act of 1989, has spread in astonishing ways to the public schools. In Hamilton, Ohio, two junior high school girls were suspended under a tough anti-drug policy after one student gave the other two Tylenol tablets for a headache, according to a *New York Times* story. That school punishes any exchange of drugs, even legal ones, and allows students to take medication only after getting permission of school officials and with an adult present.[27] Curfews and street sweeps are becoming common in Florida and Ohio; the Lawrence, Massachusetts police have been confiscating Medicaid and food stamp cards of people arrested but not yet convicted on drug charges.[28]

What has happened to the "self-evident" truth that all people have "certain unalienable rights" including life, liberty, and the pursuit of happiness? The war on drugs has, in too many cases, tried to obscure that evidence and has encouraged attitudes and laws that we might someday—perhaps a soon day—regret.

In summary of goals, national drug policy should

- minimize the risks to physical and mental health of drug users and their family members;
- contribute to sustaining the quality of neighborhood life and safety of the streets;
- encourage efficient allocations of resources designed to alleviate drug-use problems and the reduction of current economic and social costs of the drug problem;
- recognize and exploit the advantages inherent in the acceptance and management of a tolerable level of recreational drug use;
- aim to reduce frictions between the United States and other countries, and contribute to the development of countries now involved in the drug problem; and
- enhance the moral quality of relationships between American citizens and the organs of government.

A NEW POLICY

Before presenting explicit recommendations for a new policy, it will be helpful to reiterate some basic points made earlier.

First, a major premise in American democracy is that individual persons ought both to be free to choose what they do with their lives and to bear major responsibility for the consequences of those choices; people are assumed to be moral agents. In the context of the drug problem, this means that drug use represents an explicit behavior choice under particular circumstances. It means that people are acting as people have for millenia to achieve states of satisfaction or pleasure by means that supplement those making up the bulk of life's pursuits. The fact that a person starts or stops drug use in particular circumstances and for particular reasons as part of the process of making it through life requires that we abandon the adversarial view of a drug as a "thing," "inherently evil in itself," to be "fought" by means of a "war on drugs."

Nelson Rockefeller epitomized this wrong view in his effort to exploit public fear and ignorance of drugs in a campaign to retain his governorship of New York. Speaking of his opponent, Rockefeller said, "Frank O'Connor's election would mean that narcotic addicts would continue to be free to roam the streets—to mug, snatch purses, steal, even murder, or to spread the deadly infection that affects them possibly to your son or daughter. Half the crime in New York City is committed by narcotic addicts."[29] How simple-minded (or devious?) must politicians become in the pursuit of office?

The war on drugs is more accurately described as a war on people who may choose to use certain drugs. It violates the fundamental common law principle that people are responsible for their actions. By punishing people for simply possessing drugs, prohibition acts in anticipation of people doing things that might harm others, whether or not the doing actually happens or harm actually results.

A second major point is that it is the duty of government in America to act so as to enhance individual freedom congruent with the objective of maximizing freedom for all citizens. This step requires a degree of regulation imposing constraints on behavior such that exercizing one's own freedom does not infringe the freedoms of others—a juggling act of no mean dimensions, but one that is represented in a vast array of public policies and laws, from anti-trust legislation to building safety codes, speed limits, parking rules, and motorcycle safety helmets. In the context of the drug problem, this means that we must recognize the possibility of compulsive uses of drugs in ways that may harm others, and devise regulations that will afford protection of the public while not over-restricting the behavior of people who choose to use drugs. Examples abound: driving automobiles under the influence of alcohol kills more people annually than does the use of all illegal drugs combined; improved management of alcohol use is clearly needed. Sickness and death from lung cancer brought on by nicotine addiction impose massive costs on other taxpayers and insurance rate-payers, not to mention the suffering and economic costs born directly by the families of the "prematurely dead"; we can do a better job of managing nicotine consumption. More directly for drug policy, it means that we should search for ways to manage drug use so as to reduce the costs imposed on others while still allowing people to make the choice to use drugs.

Thus I present the drug policy that I would like ultimately to see in effect—after years of preparing the public through education and experimentation. It is clearly representative of a public health orientation, one that is well stated by Steven Jonas, a physician and professor of preventive medicine: "to reduce and control the use of all the recreational mood-altering drugs in order to provide for their safe, pleasurable use, consistent with centuries-old human experience, while minimizing their harmful effects on individuals, the family, and society as a whole."[30] In its broadest form, my proposal is hopelessly consistent and recklessly comprehensive and would meet formidable resistance from powerful economic and political interests from the start, but as a beginning I propose that

1. All recreational drugs—specifically, heroin, alcohol, cocaine, nicotine, and marijuana—would be available in a regulated open market.
2. All forms of advertising and other promotion would be maximally restricted within constitutional limits.
3. Legal regulation would be in the form of licensure for both sellers and buyers, combined with a system for keeping records of sales.
   (a) Citizens could apply for licenses on reaching the age of 18 and would be required to demonstrate knowledge of how drugs work and how to use them safely, and of the risks of unsafe use (similar to automobile licensing practices in most states).
   (b) Courts would be empowered to suspend purchasers' licenses based on evidence of law violations (e.g., assault, driving under the influence, robbery, vagrancy, malicious mischief) attributable to excessive use. Other sentences for these offenses would continue in effect as at present. Fines or other punishments would apply in cases of unlicensed buying or selling.
   (c) Sellers' licenses would also be revoked for selling to under age or unlicensed buyers, followed by appropriate punishment.
4. Minimal quality control standards would be established by the Food and Drug Administration and the Department of Agriculture to protect against impurities; packages would contain information on contents, and warnings against over-use.
5. Price regulation would be left to market processes.
6. Federal taxes would apply uniformly to each class of product. State and local taxes would be applied at the discretion of the jurisdiction, with the objective of taxing to a limit below that which would encourage the emergence of black markets.

7. Proceeds from taxes on the sale of regulated drugs would be directed toward the following:
   (a) monitoring the use of drugs and problems that might arise therefrom, specifically including research on drug policy;
   (b) research on improved methods of treatment and for prevention of overuse; and
   (c) programs for treatment in appropriate settings and educational programs for prevention of excessive drug use, in schools, churches, other appropriate settings, and the media generally.
8. Funds in amounts formerly allocated to the domestic "war on drugs" would be dedicated to programs of human development having objectives of providing potential drug abusers with alternatives, including improved education generally, specific job training and such other programs as research and ingenuity might suggest.
9. Funds in amounts formerly allocated to the "war on drugs" as pursued outside U.S. borders would be assigned as guided by general foreign policy interests to programs of international development.

Let us consider some of the objections to the substance of such a policy, setting aside for the moment the mere practical problems confronting any legalization proposals.

As for the first, second, and third proposals, it may not be necessary to struggle against the nicotine interests toward stronger regulation, in view of the progress that has been made over the last twenty years in reducing cigarette smoking through programs of health education and propaganda. Surely both the alcohol and nicotine interests would fiercely oppose the degree of regulation suggested. Very likely the consumers of nicotine and alcohol products would dislike the additional burden of licensure and the recording of sales in a market wherein they are free to place others at risk and abuse themselves at will. I can foresee "invasion of privacy" objections to any record-keeping proposal even though we hear none about today's recording of sales of legally prescribable narcotics, such as Percodan and Demerol, or of prescription drugs in general.

As for the fourth proposal, the Food and Drug Administration is an already burdened regulatory agency and might resist additional duties unless strongly led, fully funded, and backed by public opinion and specific legislation. Resistance might be aided by the drug manufacturing and marketing industry, which now largely controls the supply of research data on which regulatory decisions are based.

Being Practical About Changing Policy

My suspicion is that the most practical approach to a policy legalizing presently illicit drugs would be to continue the hypocrisy about nicotine and alcohol, hoping for the best from present health education efforts, and concentrate on the potential benefits of gradually relaxing the controls on marijuana, heroin, cocaine, and their various forms and derivatives. Thus the policy recommended as a ten-year target would be the one stated above, but with references to nicotine and alcohol removed. This would probably be far more acceptable to the third drug culture, that is, the tobacco smoking and alcohol drinking public and to the smoking and drinking legislators and executives they elect. Remember, illicit drug users of almost any degree are usually seen as different from the rest of us or even dangerous, and should have to put up with licensure, recording of sales, and heavy taxes if they are to be allowed to pursue their (bad) forms of seeking gratification.

To make clearer the possible cost savings from legalization, I have prepared Table 6.1, using arbitrary estimates of decreases and increases in the classes of costs presented in Chapter 2. Even if the net gains suggested in this table are off by half, significant sums would be available for more positive anti-drug actions than the war on drugs now gives us.

The Test Is in the Details

Alas, nothing is as simple as it at first appears. And managing a policy such as I have recommended would be anything but simple—given the differences between drugs and their effects, the different user populations, and the many options available for regulating the use and distribution of drugs. A great deal of thought has gone into how the details of a liberalized drug policy might work, and we can thank Richard Karel for a very useful summary.[31] Looking first at production, a legally produced drug could be subjected to strict standards of purity and cleanliness via the Department of Agriculture and the Food and Drug Administration, not to mention the product quality incentives in the free market. As we have noted elsewhere, to establish coca, opium, and cannabis as cash crops could produce major economic advantages. It would reduce the need for some farm subsidies, generate jobs for farmers, chemists, retailers, and others in the production-distribution chain as well as provide an expansion of the tax base.

As for distribution, the government's role would be solely as regulator, not distributor. Karel's suggestions appear to rely heavily on the physician-

Table 6.1

Potential Economic Savings from Legalization (in millions of $)

Reductions in "other related costs" [a]		From	To	Saving
Crime expenditures	(-75%)	13,203	3,300	9,903
Private legal expense	(-75%)	1,381	345	1,036
Victims of crime	(-75%)	842	210	632
Incarceration	(-80%)	4,434	887	3547
Crime careers	(-80%)	13,976	2679	10,717
Other Federal cost reductions [b]				
Interdiction costs	(-100%)	2,200	0	2,200
International anti-drug	(-25%)	768	384	384
OCDETF [c]	(-90%)	399	40	359
ONDCP ("Czar") [d]	(-75%)	69	17	52
Sub-total				28,830
Less: Increase in prevention, research, and service [e]				3,572
Sub-total				25,258
Less: Increase in treatment, research, and services [e]				2,802
Sub-total				22,456
Plus: Net income from drug taxes [f]				15,000
Grand total savings				**$37,456**

[a] See Rice et al., 1990 [b] OMB, U.S. Budget Fiscal Year 1993 [c] Organized Crime Drug Enforcement Task Force [d] Office of National Drug Control Policy. From 1992 budget; not specified in 1993 budget summary [e] Heuristic proposal [f] Various sources; amount could vary with method

pharmacist relationship, but regulated distribution could be effected through other relationships. Chewing gum, candies, and smokeable fibers or granules with known drug content could be made available to addicts through existing pharmaceutical outlets, and distribution to addicts controlled through a physician-prescription system. Certain drugs that may have relatively higher risks of addiction, or may be dangerous to psychologically unstable people, but which have considerable positive potential when properly used, such as LSD and MDMA, would be especially good candidates for control through a physician prescription system, and assigned to a protective classification analogous to Schedule III or IV under current law.

Beverages containing small defined amounts of coca as well as coca tea could be treated as foodstuffs. Being non-addictive, marijuana could be sold with minor regulation through tobacco shops. (On the other hand, perhaps marijuana should not risk having its emerging reputation contaminated by association with what is already our most dangerously addictive drug.) Regulated distribution of other drugs could be effected through the use of a card similar to the familiar Automatic Teller Machine card. If the record shows that insufficient time has elapsed since the card carrier's last purchase, the vendor would be obligated to refuse sale. Circumvention of this control system would be possible, no doubt, but it would be better than forcing the user into a criminal market as we do today.

Under a fully reformed policy, random drug testing would have to be abandoned and replaced by a system of performance sampling on jobs having significant public health or public safety implications and for which a clear relationship between drug use and performance has been established.

In the next and final chapter, we will look more closely at the ways and means of bringing about change.

Chapter 7

Getting There from Here

Are there significant prospects for making U.S. drug policy less restrictive? One of my colleagues believes that legalization is an idea whose time has come, that it will be backed in the next five years by liberals and conservatives alike, but for different reasons. Many conservatives, he argues, will become incensed by the high, and still rising, costs of law enforcement and incarceration. Hearing continued public concern about raising taxes, the conservatives will join a reform movement temporarily (and possibly unwittingly) with liberals who are pursuing the agenda of both civil liberties and cost containment in backing decriminalization and eventually legalization positions, which are complete with provisions for taxation targeted for increased treatment and prevention.

But be wary, he warns: once legalization is a fact, ordinary politics, and fiscal imperatives led by a power elite recognized by government administrators, will see to it that the taxes from drug sales are diverted from treatment and prevention into the general fund and thence to wherever the political process sends them. He cites the failure of the community mental health legislation of 1963 and onward, which promised "de-institutionalization" of hospitalized mental patients to the care of comprehensive centers in their home communities. Then the financial demands of the Vietnam War prevented the fulfillment of President Kennedy's original dream. Fewer than one-third of the planned centers were created, and now a third of the homeless are discharged mental hospital patients. My colleague fears this sort of thing could happen again. What constituency concerned for the one-time drug users is vocal enough to ensure that the drug-use problem is dealt with? Surely not the drug users: their part of the national demography does not vote much and does not lobby legislators. "To hell with 'em" will become the conservative position, and it will prevail, he fears.

Opposing this pessimistic, even cynical view, is the position that one must have hope and that in the long run truth, reason, and even compassion, can prevail over ignorance, rigidity and fear. There is a large and growing number of individual scholars and organizations of concerned citizens who are working through education, exhortation, and political persuasion to develop and argue the case for a more economical and enlightened approach to the drug problem. They are far from unanimous in their preferred solutions and in the particular aspects of the problem that attract their interests and energies. All agree on the urgency of the need for reform. Some simply advocate some degree or form of legalization; too few offer recommendations on how to bring it about, seeming often to ignore the complexity of the problem and the formidable economic and political forces of the second and third drug cultures, not to mention the ignorance and the deep-seated and widely held fears that lie in the way of a new policy. The most active and influential of reformist organizations are represented in Appendix B, Reform-Oriented Organizations.

In addition to these continuing interest groups, government agencies and foundations have sponsored special committees and commissions of broadly representative and usually impartial experts to shed light on drug-related issues of their day. The results of fourteen such studies have been summarized by the Drug Policy Foundation and are presented with the foundation's permission as Appendix C.

OBSTACLES AND OPPORTUNITIES TO CHANGE

Drug policy, like every public policy, exists in, and gains its validity from, political consensus. It can only be changed by changing that consensus. And that takes time, work, and wisdom in pursuing a political contest. Winning any contest means knowing your opposition, both strengths and weaknesses; so let us make note of the major forces to be dealt with in seeking to change drug policy; these are the second and third of the three drug cultures first described in Chapter 1.

The second drug culture is the formidable array of political and organizational forces that make up the war on drugs and would stand to lose as a result of legalization or anything approaching it. As we noted in Chapter 3, from one perspective of the drug warriors, the war has been a smashing success: appropriations have increased, more people have been hired, jobs of managers have been upgraded, missions have been broadened, public praise has been bestowed, and legislators and prosecutors have been re-elected for being "tough on drugs." In effect these people are saying, "We are doing our job, our careers are secure, we're busting traffickers and arresting dealers and jailing users; what more could one ask?" In addition to organizational drug warriors and their elected allies, there is also the array of academics, journalists, and propagandists like the Partnership for a Drug-Free America, whose work depends at least partly on the drug war in its present form. Finally, let us not forget the health insurance, health care and drug testing industries, all of which would be faced with major changes should drug law reform set in. Any effort to reform drug policy would have to deal directly with these forces. That is why reform can only move slowly; the government's anti-drug organizations, built up over the decades, probably cannot be, nor should they be, quickly dismantled. After all, they are comprised very largely of good people sincerely committed to their work, and should be the beneficiaries of efforts to provide alternative careers as policy evolves.

The third drug culture embodies the bulk of the public that eschews illicit drugs, but uses all kinds of licit recreational drugs plus prescription and over-the-counter preparations in the interest of feeling good. This drug culture, reminiscent of the shadows of class conflict in the drug war described by John Helmer[1] and Clarence Lusane,[2] harbors exaggeratedly fearful attitudes about illicit drugs, based largely on a lack of information and the residue of indoctrination about drug terrors over the past seventy years. Continued education through means recommended in detail later in this chapter may gradually allay this fear and open the way for effective political action.

Legal and Constitutional Issues

In seeking to revise so deeply ingrained a policy and set of attitudes as that which represents today's criminalization of drugs, one must accept and emphasize patience and gradualness as ingredients of reformist action, for there is yet no strong demand for a sharp break from the drug war prohibitionist mentality, as there was during the late 1920s and early '30s for repealing the prohibition of the sale of alcoholic drinks.[3] Moreover, a move to change the current federal orientation quickly would undoubtedly encounter a thicket of constitutional issues involving the Constitution's commerce clause (Article I, Section 8), states' rights, and privacy, to mention but three.

I suggest, therefore, the adoption of a moderate long-range goal akin to the adoption of the Twenty-first Amendment, and with initial focus on removing marijuana from the list of federally controlled substances and assigning its regulation to the states. Remember, that amendment in repealing the Eighteenth Amendment did not directly legalize the alcoholic beverage industry. It simply turned the legalization decision over to the states, capitalizing on the strong tradition of states' rights. The legal framework for doing this is partially in effect now, as shown in the fact that several states already have acted to de-criminalize—partly through reduced enforcement—the possession of marijuana for personal use. Even though possession remains a violation of federal law, enforcement is mostly left to the states, in keeping with the constitutionally established tradition of limiting federal law enforcement to matters primarily affecting commerce between the states. It is thus possible for a state to say, in effect, "Okay, marijuana possession is still against federal law, but if you feds want it enforced, send in your marshalls, deputize—and pay—our expanded police forces and quadruple the number of federal courts. Our police and courts have more urgent business."

Of course, the situation is much more complicated than I have suggested, for federal practices have made it difficult for states to avoid cooperation with federal policies. States have adopted prohibitionary statutes paralleling federal laws, persuaded in part by the threat of losing federal highway funds for their own road development programs—much as Mexico has been threatened with economic sanctions unrelated to drug issues as persuasion to cooperate more enthusiastically in our drug war.

Nonetheless, this relationship between federal and state law is what makes it reasonable for the New York State legislature to consider a bill introduced in 1989 by Senator Joseph Galiber that would repeal all provisions of current law that designate specified substances and their possession and sale as illegal, and would allow the sale without prescription of substances formerly illegal through specially licensed pharmacists and physicians.[4] To no one's surprise, that bill went nowhere in the 1989 legislative session. Senator Galiber in 1991 introduced a similar bill dealing only with marijuana; at this writing the bill remains committed to the Senate's Committee on Investigations, Taxation, and Government Operations, and will be reintroduced in the 1992–93 legislative session.

In a thoughtful book appraising and criticizing America's efforts to cope with the drug problem, Daniel Benjamin and Roger Miller have specifically called for turning the problem over to state authority, much like what occurred with the ending of alcohol prohibition after the repeal of the Eighteenth Amendment. Noting that the Twenty-first Amendment simply left the decisions about alcohol to the states and through the states to subordinate jurisdictions, these writers call for a similar approach to the drug problem, and name their position "The Constitutional Alternative."[5] Although these writers appear to favor a broadly permissive national policy, the thrust of their argument is that drug law would be more responsive to citizens' wishes were the full authority to be returned to the states, with the states and the jurisdictions within them opting for any desired degree of stringency or leniency in drug law and policy. And being responsible for financing whatever policy is adopted would surely focus state and local attention on drug-related issues. Their position is interesting and deserves debate within the community of drug policy reformers.

In calling for a delegation of regulatory power over drugs to the states, Benjamin and Miller express a fear that the federal government would, through an act legalizing currently illicit drugs, mandate the absence of state regulation and thus create an unwanted condition in which people have no choice but to live in a community where drugs were legal in all respects. It is indeed possible under the Constitution for Congress to "occupy the field" in a particular realm of policy, and thus preempt the authority of the states to regulate practices within it. That is just what has been done in the field of anti-drug law. In showing that occupation of the field is not done casually, Laurence Tribe's analysis[6] quotes from a 1963 Supreme Court decision:

> The principle to be derived from [the Supreme Court's] decisions is that federal regulation of a field of commerce should not be deemed preemptive of state regulatory power in the absence of persuasive reasons—either that the nature of the regulated subject matter permits no other conclusion, or that the Congress has unmistakably so ordained.[7]

Given the present federal preemption of the field, and noting that Congress is made up of people representing the states, it seems unlikely in the extreme that in tempering current prohibitions of drugs Congress would try to mandate the absence of a state's regulation of its own internal commerce.

Procedurally, Benjamin and Miller assert that basic reform could be accomplished by amending the Comprehensive Drug Abuse and Control Act of 1970 to return all authority for control of psychoactive drugs to the states, and they offer two ways of doing it. One would be to repeal certain sections of the act and insert a section drawn directly from the Twenty-First Amendment: "The transportation or importation into any state, territory, or possession of the United States for delivery or use therein of any controlled substance, in violation of the laws thereof, is hereby prohibited." The other would revise section 903 of the act, which asserted federal "occupancy of the field," such that the Federal Government relinquishes occupancy: "Any conflict between that provision of this subchapter and that state law so that the two cannot stand together shall be resolved by construing the law so as to give full effect to the relevant state law."[8]

There may be alternative forms of federal withdrawal from the present aggressive pursuit of the drug problem, with different combinations of residual powers in the central government and guidelines to the states, but the initial effect of any would be to return much of the responsibility for coping with the problem to state and local authority.

As has been noted earlier, the U.S.'s obligations under the United Nation's Single Convention on Narcotic Drugs could be eliminated in six months by invoking Article 46 of the convention.

Education and Advocacy

In the shorter run, I believe that educational and political action objectives should concentrate on one drug at a time, because the user populations of the three principal illegals are different, the mechanisms of their action are different, and their behavioral effects are different. John Flynn argues that to lump all currently illegal drugs into a big bad category called "drugs of abuse" is to invite confusion and to frustrate attempts to deal rationally with what is actually a multiple-drug problem, not just "the drug problem." Compare marijuana and cocaine for an illustration: (1) they differ vastly in potential for addiction, with marijuana having virtually none; (2) consequences of abuse are very different, with the cocaine user more likely to use drug injection and suffer the consequences of diseases unknown to those who restrict their drug use to marijuana; and (3) the prospects of experiencing a serious medical emergency with marijuana are tiny compared to cocaine.[9]

Given the masses of information with which the public is constantly assaulted, it would be just asking too much to aim early toward an across-the-board legalization. Marijuana would seem to be the choice for early concentration, for it is gradually coming to be seen by authorities and scholars of the drug problem less and less as a threat to sanity and health.[10]

The experience enjoyed thus far in states where marijuana has been de-criminalized should be constantly monitored, analyzed, and publicized. That experience could also provide the basis for interesting simulation research on consequences of loosening controls on marijuana in other circumstances. Thanks to the National Organization for the Reform of

Marijuana Laws (NORML), there is an extensive literature arguing the economic benefits of resuming the commercial cultivation of hemp, both as a source of fiber for cloth, paper, and other products made from wood, and as a renewable source of energy from clean burning fuel.

We have also accumulated a body of knowledge on heroin and cocaine use and how such use is affected by price, by the risks of arrest, or by opportunities for having a decent life and self-respect in the absence of such mood-altering drugs. Thus, we have a data base that could be used in simulation experiments to feel out the possible effects of changes in law as it particularly affects uses of those drugs.

Nearly all advocates of reform are believers that multiple forms, sites, and use of media for education must be vigorously pursued. Above all, educational efforts about drugs themselves must be credible, recognizing that people take drugs because they want to feel good, and that they will take drugs responsibly when they can see that it is in their own best interests to do so. Drug facts and arguments about public policy can be presented in public forums at all levels, national certainly, but more importantly at the grass-roots level, in order to promote citizen interaction, understanding, and involvement. Interested citizens can involve local government, schools, colleges, police, courts, medical societies, and social services and write letters to the editors of newspapers and magazines nationwide. Much of the point of this activity is to establish the fact that thoughtful people believe differently about the nature of the drug problem from what the drug warriors would have us believe, that there are other reasonable ways to deal with drugs beyond the ways of the warriors, and that "the drug problem" itself need not be seen to be as frightening as traditional views would have it.

Illustrative of ways to promote and provoke constructive discussion and analysis of the issues is the set of bills that have been introduced into various state legislatures—in Pennsylvania, Missouri, Massachusetts, Oregon, and New York, with two bills—to regulate and tax the sale of marijuana. These bills have been summarized by attorney Richard Evans, who was also a member of a group of lawyers, economists, and other specialists in drug issues called the National Task Force on Cannabis Regulation.[11] Sponsored by NORML, this group researched and then drafted a federal bill entitled The Cannabis Revenue Act, which had the following goals for cannabis policy: (1) to control marijuana abuse; (2) to protect public health; (3) to eliminate the illicit market in cannabis and the crime associated with it; (4) to produce new revenue; and (5) to remove legal obstacles to the emergence of a new hemp industry. Another and much broader bill drafted for introduction into the U.S. House of Representatives in 1989 would repeal current federal prohibition laws and allow states wide latitude in regulating drug use, but would deny federal funds to states flatly prohibiting drug trade. Nonetheless, the proposal contained serious drawbacks, including permission for states to impose major penalties and restrictions, that antagonized a broad spectrum of people concerned with drug policy. It was never introduced.

The admirable educational efforts being conducted by experienced organizations specifically devoted to drug policy reform deserve the support of all reform-minded individuals. The Drug Policy Foundation has created a series of more than forty professionally produced educational videos, which it offers as America's Drug Forum, for use in schools, libraries, and other public settings; the series is broadcast annually by a large number of PBS television stations. The National Organization for the Reform of Marijuana Laws has an extensive library of documents available for general use. Other advocacy groups are the Religious Coalition for a Moral Drug Policy, Families Against Mandatory Minimums, and the Criminal Justice Policy Foundation. Still others and their addresses are listed in Appendix B, Reform-Oriented Organizations.

The classic method for effecting policy change in our democracy is through the ballot box. Pete McCloskey, a former Republican Congressman addressing National Drug Strategy Network's meeting at the Drug Policy Foundation's fifth international conference on drug policy reform in November 1991, told activists that there is indeed hope for reform through legislation if the right tactics are used. McCloskey stressed the importance of urging incumbents and candidates to commit themselves on a few simple issues, like "Yes, the dollar cost of keeping drug users in prison must be cut," and then letting legislators know that there is a voting constituency out there that they should listen to. McCloskey wisely said, "You won't get the government to act, no matter how hard you just implore. The potential consequences of the legislator's action or non-action—are what count."

Therefore, a target deserving special educational attention consists of state legislators and members of Congress. In spite of the appearance of stupidity in much of what transpires in our state and national legislatures, there are hundreds of legislators who are open to new ideas and willing to respond to thoughtful arguments, especially if the arguments are not of the simplistic sort that can be handled by instructing an aide to "answer this fellow with the Form b-3 letter." Again I point to NORML and its numerous chapters around the country as sources of advice on how to approach legislators on various aspects of drug law reform.

I add that it is important for legislators to hear not only from groups with organizational names and purporting to represent large numbers of voters, but also from individual citizens. Legislators are all too familiar with political gamesmanship of pressure groups, like leagues, unions, association, coalitions, or citizens for or against one thing or another, and look skeptically at an unfamiliar letterhead as the work of another peculiar pressure group. An accumulation of letters from Joe Doakes, mechanic, Mary Smith, beautician, and Henry Kowalski, barber, paints a picture of sincere lay-person concern and tells the legislator that it is safe to take a stand on drug law reform. It is also important to remember that most legislators are followers—of constituent pressure groups and individual citizens—not leaders. Re-election is the main objective toward which their days are directed—and not altogether cynically. They cannot afford to promote unpopular issues. A legislator needs to know she will have support if she is to go to bat for any cause. After all, a legislator says, "No matter what good cause I believe in in my heart, I can't do it a bit of good if I'm not in office."

What should be the content of such educational efforts? It is important to base drug policy reform arguments clearly on already accepted values, emphasizing the validity of their connection with drug reform. Among these arguments are the right to control what happens to one's body—a theme now clearly stated in hospitals and other health care settings: you are in control; you may refuse this treatment if you choose. With respect to drugs, people should be allowed to make bad decisions as well as good ones, and suffer the consequences, just as they do in business, the professions, and in families. Another argument is the right of privacy—the capacity to control what information about oneself that others may have. The growing trend toward drug testing—to find out if someone has used a drug in the recent past as contrasted with capacity to perform a job—or to be searched or asked about drug possession simply on "suspicion" is truly destructive of this right.

Here are a few other suggestions, not necessarily in order of importance: First, there should be a major "de-bunking" of the terrors of the drug scene, particularly attending to a drug singled out for special attention. By this I mean not a denial of the health and safety risks in drug use, but a cool and careful presentation of many well-established facts: for example, (1) cocaine use is not automatically and instantly addictive; (2) drug habits can be broken voluntarily, especially when there is something more attractive to do in one's life; (3) health risks of heroin come mainly from the use of illegal and dirty needles and from chemical contaminants, not from heroin itself; (4) marijuana effects are moderate at worst, non-addictive generally; and (5) marijuana is not a "gateway drug" that leads inevitably to more hazardous drugs. The literature available for education along these lines is rich and well founded on scientific research. Reason can often prevail in the relative quiet of legislative committee work.

Next could be a questioning of the economic costs and the general effectiveness of the war on drugs. This should have strong appeal to people concerned with holding down taxes, containing costs, or even avoiding having a prison built "in my back yard."

And apart from just mitigating the bad side effects of the drug war, a reasonable claim can be made that, under legalization, positive benefits can be realized from the careful and informed use of some drugs that are now illegal. In making his case for legalization, Richard Miller elaborates on this point, noting that heroin can calm rowdy teenagers and help adolescents through a difficult time of life, help neurotics hold jobs and get along better with people, that cocaine in small and controlled amounts can relieve depression and anxiety, and improve athletic performance and other work requiring stamina over long hours.[12]

Possibly of greatest long-run importance would be challenging in the courts the continuing, even the expanding, risks that the drug war imposes on civil liberties and other values basic to U.S. society. The American Civil Liberties Union does a heroic job within its limited means of monitoring court cases that infringe the civil liberties of particular plaintiffs or appellants and legislation that would generally put civil liberties at greater risk. Such work also deserves the support and active participation of reform-minded people.

Ingenuity of the serious reform-minded person will discover more arguments and themes than it would be profitable to try to lay out here. As a useful guide, the Drug Policy Foundation has published a *National Drug Reform Strategy* in booklet form which can be obtained from the Foundation. In summary, the strategy aims to:

- reverse drug policy funding priorities, which now provide 70 percent of federal funds for law enforcement and 30 percent for prevention;
- curtail AIDS by making clean needles available to addicts who take drugs intravenously;
- develop a plan for drug treatment on demand, allow Medicaid to pay for treatment for poor people, and expand the variety of treatment options available;
- stop prosecutions of pregnant drug users, and expand drug treatment and prenatal care as a means of reducing the problems of drug-exposed infants;

- make medical marijuana available to people who are seriously ill; and
- appoint a commission to examine seriously alternatives to drug prohibition.

FINALLY

The drug problem as it is most commonly perceived and the drug war as it is waged are problems with symptoms in many areas and institutions—neighborhoods, families, courts, prisons, military services, foreign relations, hospitals and clinics, budget offices, laboratories, social services, schools, and churches. Fundamentally, the drug problem arises from the private human problem of seeking satisfaction and pleasure in life, but it becomes a prime public problem in large part through the shortage of opportunities for the discovery of more constructive pleasures and rewards. The precipitating reason for the "scourge of drugs" is the political institution of law, which must be adapted to recognize that the human search for pleasure and personal fulfillment cannot be stopped, and that the use of drugs in that search can be regulated in ways that will strike a proper balance between social order and individual freedom.

Appendix A

Federal Drug Laws

If a well-educated non-lawyer wants to develop a thorough understanding of federal legislation bearing on licit or illicit drugs, that person should be prepared to set aside several months to be devoted to little else. Of great value would be addictions to de-coding convoluted prose, to tracing relations between laws and their later amendments and repeals, and to studying the byzantine interactions among congressional committees and with their acolytes, constituents, and sycophants. But short of that, even a modest insight into drug legislation will initiate an appreciation of the sometimes mind-boggling complexity of the nation's drug problem and the war being waged against it. Part of the beauty of our democracy is the intricate lace that our legislators weave in what they assert to be the public good. I have eschewed this particular esthetic experience and instead have relied on the dedicated work of other professionals in preparing the following introduction to federal drug legislation, notably scholars in the Congressional Research Service of the Library of Congress, and those who keep Section 21 of the U.S. Code up to date.

For openers, I report that at least eighty-two federal laws have been enacted since 1961 that relate at least in some significant part to the drug problem, not counting international treaties and their amendments. These laws are identified by Congress number and serial number within that Congress. For example, **The Drug Abuse Control Amendments of 1965** were enacted by the Eighty-ninth Congress, given number 74, and entered into history as **P.L. [Public Law] 89–74**.

A good many of these laws do not have drugs as a major focus, but take a passing swipe at some drug-related problem: **P.L. 96–528, the Agriculture Appropriations Act for 1981**, deals only slightly with drugs, prohibiting the use of appropriated funds to pay people or corporations that harvest for illegal-use marijuana or other prohibited drug-producing plants. (On the other hand, some laws that attend primarily to drugs take passing swipes at other matters, as the **Anti-Drug Abuse Act of 1986** does when it decrees in Section 12006 that states shall develop minimum uniform standards for issuing commercial drivers' licenses. This sort of activity falls under the "and for other purposes" phrase that ends the statement of purpose accompanying most major laws.)

Some of the laws I have reviewed merely extend earlier authorizations. Others, far better known to reform-minded people and those involved in any of the three drug cultures (For explanation see Chapter 1.), focus clearly and strongly on drug issues. A recent important example is **P.L. 100–690**, the **Anti-Drug Abuse Act of 1988**, with its ten titles dealing almost exclusively with drug-related problems of many kinds: treatment and prevention programs, drug abuse education and prevention, international relations, the accountability of drug users, the death penalty and other punitive enhancements, improvement of state and local narcotics control, and many others. **P.L. 100–690** is long and detailed; the summary prepared by the Congressional Research Service (CRS) runs to seventy-nine pages.

The following summary is by no means comprehensive; it omits a number of the laws currently in effect and highlights those that are most prominent. If you are interested in more details, your congressman can get them for you from the CRS, or you can visit the nearest law library and look them up in Title 21 of the U.S. Code, Sections 801 and 951, which cover food and drug laws of all kinds.

A final note before the summary: not all federal drug legislation is bad from the reformer's point of view. Many laws have excellent provisions for increased education, prevention, treatment, and research. Also, there are trends throughout the laws to move into and out of degrees of severity in the treatment of convicted offenders. Regrettably, though, much of the legislation, most notably the laws passed during the Reagan and Bush administrations beginning with **P.L. 97–86**, pushes the federal government, and state governments, toward further excesses in the war on drugs. These trends are seen particularly in more infringements of civil liberties, extentions of the power of the military in enforcing domestic law, and by pushing minor first-time offenders to the fringes of society by stigmatizing them with criminal records and sending them to criminal socializing institutions we outsiders call prisons. Thus, because of the bias of this book, the summaries will highlight features of the law that reform-minded people find most offensive.

P.L. 89–74, Drug Abuse Control Amendments of 1965: This law amends the Food, Drug, and Cosmetic Act to provide for special controls over the manufacture and distribution of depressant and stimulant drugs, and to make possession of the drugs (other than by the user) illegal outside the legitimate channels of commerce.

P.L. 89–793, Narcotic Rehabilitation Act of 1966: This law provides for civil commitment, for treatment of narcotic addicts charged with federal law violations, and for civil commitment to federal care of addicts not charged with any criminal offense. It also provides for grants to states to assist in specialized services for addicts, and makes federal marijuana law violators eligible for parole.

P.L. 90–639, Increased Penalties for Dangerous Drug Offenders: This law provides increased penalties for trafficking in depressants and stimulants, and makes their possession illegal unless obtained through a valid prescription.

P.L. 91–452, Organized Crime Control Act of 1970: This comprehensive law has several titles, and much of its content deals with procedures that make it easier for the government to prosecute offenders of many kinds, including drug law offenders.

P.L. 91–513, Comprehensive Drug Abuse Prevention and Control Act of 1970: This is the sweeping legislation that made major revisions in existing policy. Its **Title II, the Controlled Substances Act**, replaced previous narcotic and dangerous drug control laws (excepting those relating to imports and exports). The major provisions of Title II are (1) establishment of the five separate schedules for classifying all narcotics and other dangerous drugs; (2) transfer to the Secretary of Health, Education, and Welfare of authority to designate the classification of substances to be controlled under the act; (3) extension of existing law's licensing requirements for narcotics manufacturers to apply to manufacturers of all controlled drugs and all distributors of the same; (4) a revision of penalties, among which is one to make any first-time, simple possession offense a misdemeanor, regardless of the drug involved; (5) possible expungement of police record after satisfactory probation following first-offense convictions; (6) making possible use of "no-knock" search warrants by officers engaged in enforcing the act; and (7) increasing federal narcotics enforcement by 300 agents plus support personnel.

P.L. 92–73, Department of Agriculture—Environmental and Consumer Protection Appropriations Act, 1972: The act contains a provision barring payment of federal subsidies to farmers who knowingly allow wild marijuana growing on their land to be harvested.

P.L. 92–226, Foreign Assistance Act of 1971: Among other things, the act authorizes suspension of assistance to countries not cooperating in attempts to control illegal drug traffic to the U.S., and creates a program designed to encourage international narcotics control.

P.L. 92–245, 92–246, and **92–247**: These laws authorize U.S. contributions to various international development banks, but each contains a provision instructing the U.S. representative to each of them to vote against any loan to any country about which the U.S. president has determined that its government has failed to take adequate steps to prevent illegal drugs from entering the United States or from being sold to any U.S. government personnel within the country's jurisdiction.

P.L. 92–255, Drug Abuse Office and Treatment Act of 1972: Title II establishes the predecessor of the modern "drug czar" in the directorship of a new Special Action Office for Drug Abuse Prevention within the executive office of the president. Though not a law enforcement agency, SAODAP was to make recommendations on enforcement and any other matters pertaining to effective conduct of any drug function.

P.L. 93–83, Crime Control Act of 1973: The law requires states receiving grants for correctional programs to provide "necessary arrangements for the development and operation of narcotic and alcoholism treatment programs in correctional institutions and facilities and in connection with probation or other supervisory release programs for all persons, incarcerated or on parole, who are addicts, alcoholics, or alcohol abusers."

P.L. 94–329, International Security Assistance and Arms Export Control Act of 1976: This law extends the provision of P.L. 92–266 for another two years, and forbids fiscal year (FY) 1976 money from going to any country where illegal traffic in opium takes place in the absence of the U.S. president's certification that the country has made progress in reducing the flow of narcotics into the United States. It also directs the president to study methods for U.S.-funded narcotics control programs in foreign countries to be assisted through international organizations.

P.L. 94–503, Crime Control Act of 1976: Among many provisions for enhancing law enforcement through the states, thet law authorizes use of federal funds for the "development of programs to identify drug-dependent offenders (including alcoholics, drug addicts, and drug abusers)," and requires the states to establish "procedures for effective coordination between state planning agencies designated under . . . the Drug Abuse Office and Treatment Act of 1972 . . . in responding to the needs of such offenders."

P.L. 96–350, Possession or Transfer of a Controlled Substance, Abroad or on the High Seas, for Import into the U.S.: Makes it unlawful for any person on board a U.S. vessel or a vessel subject to U.S. jurisdiction—or for a U.S. citizen on any vessel—to possess, manufacture, distribute, or unlawfully import a controlled substance. Also makes it unlawful for any person anywhere to possess a controlled substance intending that it will be unlawfully imported into the U.S. First offense penalties can reach fifteen years of imprisonment or a fine up to $25,000.

P.L. 97–86, Department of Defense Authorization for Appropriations for FY 1982: Among other things, by way of clarifying the Posse Comitatus statute, the law authorizes certain kinds of cooperation by the armed services with civilian law enforcement authorities for specified purposes, including enforcement of the Controlled Substances Act.

P.L. 97–113, International Security and Development Cooperation Act of 1981: This act repeals the provision of the Foreign Assistance Act that had prohibited the use of assistance funds for drug crop eradication efforts that use an herbicide shown to be harmful to human health; however, it requires the Secretary of State to notify the Secretary of Health and Human Services of any herbicide to eradicate marijuana under a program receiving assistance. The Secretary of Health and Human Services is then required to monitor the health impact of using marijuana that has been sprayed by an herbicide and to report to Congress evidence of harmful effects.

P.L. 98–164, Department of State Authorization Act, FY 1984 and FY 1985: This law extends provisions making U.S. assistance to any country that is a major producer of illegal drugs contingent on reductions by that country in levels of production. It also requires the president to submit annually a report on U.S. efforts to establish and encourage an international strategy to prevent illicit cultivation and production of, and traffic in, controlled substances.

P.L. 98–305, Controlled Substance Registrant Protection Act of 1984: This law makes it a federal crime to rob or burgle a registered dispenser of a controlled substance if (1) the replacement cost of the substance is at least $500; (2) the person committing the offense traveled interstate or in foreign commerce or used any facility in commerce to facilitate the act; or (3) another person was killed or injured as a result of the offense. Depending on circumstances, penalties of life in prison or fines of $50,000 or both may ensue.

P.L. 98– 473 (Title II), Comprehensive Crime Control Act of 1984: *Chapter III*, Forfeiture, imposes the sanction of criminal forfeiture of all drug felony offenses, and raises the ceiling to $100,000 on the value of property subject to forfeiture. *Chapter V*, Drug Enforcement Amendments, increases the maximum prison penalties for trafficking in large amounts of certain substances, and increases the level of maximum fines that may be imposed as penalties for trafficking in any controlled substance, increases penalties for trafficking in marijuana in amounts between 50 and 454 kilograms, and creates a new offense of distributing a controlled substance in or on or within a thousand feet of "the real property comprising a public or private elementary school." *Chapter IX*, Currency and Foreign Transactions Reporting Act Amendments, prohibits the attempted transport out of the U.S. of monetary instruments exceeding $10,000 without earlier filing of a report with the Treasury Department. It also allows customs officials to search, without a warrant, for unreported amounts of cash brought into or carried out of the country, and authorizes rewards to informants providing original information on a major violation of the act. *Chapter XI* makes it an offense to warn anyone that he or his property is about to be searched by federal authorities. *Chapter XII*, Procedural Amendments, authorizes emergency wiretaps without a court order under certain specified situations.

P.L. 99–570, Anti-Drug Abuse Act of 1986: This omnibus act is a far-ranging measure containing fifteen titles relating to almost every aspect of federal efforts to prevent and control the use of drugs. It provides for mandatory minimum sentences, and increases the maximums, for offenses involving larger amounts of the drugs determined as the more dangerous; extends authority to employ the armed forces to assist in civilian law enforcement; exempts from the Freedom of Information Act records compiled for law enforcement purposes that might interfere with enforcement proceedings; and authorizes the attorney general to deputize state and local law enforcement officers. Internationally, the act sets on Bolivia, Colombia, and Mexico certain conditions of drug war cooperation necessary for continuing U.S. assistance programs, and reiterates the provisions of P.L. 92–245 instructing U.S. representatives to multilateral development banks to vote against loans to countries that produce illicit drugs unless the U.S. president certifies that the country is suitably cooperating in the U.S. drug war. Under its *Title IV, Demand Reduction, sub-title B,* is the *Drug-Free Schools and Communities Act,* which authorizes major appropriations for anti-drug education throughout the country.

P.L. 100–690, Anti-Drug Abuse Act of 1988: This omnibus drug control bill contains provisions relating to virtually every aspect of the federal effort to curb abuse of narcotics and other dangerous drugs. Of ten titles, the principal concerns are with (1) new and increased penalties for offenses related to drug trafficking, the creation of new federal offenses and regulatory requirements, and changes in criminal procedures; (2) the organization and coordination of Federal anti-drug efforts; (3) the reduction of demand through increased treatment and prevention efforts; (4) the reduction of demand through increased use of sanctions against drug users; (5) the reduction of drug production abroad and of international trafficking in illicit drugs; and (6) general increases in funding authorizations and appropriations for federal drug control.

Among the provisions of special interest to reform-minded people, for various reasons, are (1) declaration of U.S. government policy to create a "drug-free America" by 1995; (2) prohibition of federal grants or contracts to any organization that does not take specified steps to provide a drug-free workplace; (3) expresses the opposition of Congress to the legalization of narcotics and other dangerous drugs; (4) affirms that Public Housing Authorities (PHAs) may evict tenants if they, or their guests, are engaged in, or convicted of, drug-related activity on or near the premises, and authorizes PHAs to investigate suspected drug law infractions; (5) identifies Peru, Colombia, Bolivia, Mexico, Pakistan, and Laos as countries to be particularly attended to with respect to their cooperation in U.S. anti-drug activities; and (6) identifies particular sums to be used in various foreign countries for drug-related activities, including military assistance, armaments and training, and safe and effective herbicides for aerial eradication of coca.

P.L. 101–647, Crime Control Act of 1990: This is another comprehensive law, having thirty-seven titles dealing with many kinds of crime and their consequences for victims and offenders alike. The law's principal drug-related provisions deal with international money laundering, drug control grants to law enforcement agencies, rural drug enforcement, drug-free school zones, putting anabolic steroids in Schedule III of the Controlled Substances Act, strengthening federal asset forfeiture authority, and establishment of voluntary shock incarceration or "boot camp" programs in the federal prison system.

Appendix B

Reform-Oriented Organizations

News media remind us with increasing frequency that there are thoughtful, reputable, and prominent people who do not believe that the way the government is trying to cope with the drug problem is the right way—that it is not morally sound, economically sensible, or, in the final analysis, effective. A recent count showed at least seventy-five organizations working in various ways toward some kind of drug law reform. A goodly number of them are state or local chapters of the oldest of them, the National Organization for the Reform of Marijuana Laws, better known as NORML. By no means do the groups have identical agendas or goals. Some groups advocate full legalization of all drugs; some concentrate on certain drugs; some promote particular issues in the drug debate; some attend primarily to legal process; some provide back-up services to others. The groups have two things in common: They all believe that liberalization of drug policy is necessary and important. None actually advocates the use of recreational drugs of any kind. Here is an alphabetical listing of the most active groups. Some commentary on several of them follows.

ALLIANCE FOR CANNABIS THERAPEUTICS, P.O. Box 21210, Kalorama Station, Washington, DC 20009.

AMERICAN CIVIL LIBERTIES UNION, 132 West 43d St., New York, NY 10036

CALIFORNIA NORML, 2215R Market St. #278, San Francisco, CA 94114.

CANNABIS ACTION NETWORK, P.O. Box 54528, Lexington, KY 40555.

CLERGY FOR ENLIGHTENED DRUG POLICY, St. Luke's Methodist Church, Wisconsin Ave. and Calvert Street NW, Washington, DC 20007.

CRIMINAL JUSTICE POLICY FOUNDATION, 2000 L St. NW, Suite 702, Washington, DC 20036.

DRUG POLICY FOUNDATION, 4455 Connecticut Ave. NW, Suite B-500, Washington, DC 20008.

FAMILIES AGAINST MANDATORY MINIMUMS (FAMM), 1001 Pennsylvania Ave. NW, Suite 200 South, Washington, DC 20004.

INTERNATIONAL ANTI-PROHIBITIONIST LEAGUE, c/o Marie-Andre Bertrand, P.O. Box 6128, University of Montreal, Criminology Department, Montreal, Quebec HC3 3S7, Canada.

LIBERTARIAN PARTY, 1528 Pennsylvania Ave. SE, Washington, DC 20003.

NATIONAL DRUG STRATEGY NETWORK, 2000 L St. NW, Suite 702, Washington, DC 20036.

NATIONAL ORGANIZATION FOR THE REFORM OF MARIJUANA LAWS, 1636 R St. NW, Washington, DC 20009.

RELIGIOUS COALITION FOR A MORAL DRUG POLICY, 3421 M St. NW, Washington, DC 20007.

The National Organization for the Reform of Marijuana Laws was founded in 1970. It provides the public with current verifiable information about marijuana, the laws relating to marijuana, and the effects they have on American society. NORML responds to requests for information about marijuana from all interested parties. Local chapters work to educate the public and to publicize NORML's services. The Washington office of NORML maintains an extensive library on all aspects of marijuana, including the legal history of marijuana, marijuana's position in the drug wars, health and medical aspects of marijuana, and other subjects. It publishes *The Drug Law Report*, a periodical that monitors the evolution of law about drugs and related court actions.

The National Drug Strategy Network is an association of individuals and organizations working against the "punitive and militaristic aspects of the 'War on Drugs'." The Network provides its members with a bi-monthly forum to exchange and develop ideas, and rapid access to relevant information through a bi-monthly newsletter, *NEWSBRIEFS*. Bi-monthly meetings in Washington focus on setting priorities and on responding to current events and information. Members meet with congressional leaders and administration officials to press the case for change, and frequently testify at state legislature and congressional hearings.

The Drug Policy Foundation describes itself as an international forum for drug policy alternatives, and emphasizes education and scholarship on the full range of drug issues. Its Sixth International Conference, held in Washington in November 1992 was attended by several hundred interested parties from all over the world—scholars, politicians, journalists, physicians, students, lawyers, social workers, and just interested others. The proceedings, consisting of sixty competitively screened presentations, are available on request, as are the proceedings of the earlier conferences. The foundation produces a weekly half-hour television series, "America's Drug Forum," seen on Public Broadcasting Stations and cable outlets; cassettes are available from the foundation.

Families Against Mandatory Minimums (FAMM) is a national organization of citizens working to repeal statutory minimum sentences through publications, seminars, and legislative advocacy. FAMM emphasizes the injustice and the high social and economic costs of mandatory minimum sentences, which the group says strip judges of power to determine fairness of sentences based on particular circumstances, and have other practical and ethical disadvantages. FAMM is a relatively new organization, but has at this writing developed branch organizations in thirteen states.

The Religious Coalition for a Moral Drug Policy is a pan-denominational organization of clergy who, through various churches and other religious organizations, disseminate information on many aspects of the nation's drug problem. Of particular concern are the moral and religious implications of actions that are pursued under the guise of winning the war on drugs. A recent publication, *Reason, Compassion, and the Drug War: A Statement by Religious Men and Women* can be obtained from the coalition.

The Criminal Justice Policy Foundation promotes understanding of the problems facing the criminal justice system and aids policy makers and the public in actions to prevent crime and improve the quality of justice. The foundation's specific activities include supporting research and writing, participating in seminars and public education programs, and providing testimony before legislative committees. The foundation also provides consultation to other organizations with kindred interests, both within and without "the establishment."

Appendix C

Studies by Special Committees, Councils, and Commissions

With the exception of the summary of the 1980 report of the directors of the Drug Abuse Council, all of the following material was prepared by the Drug Policy Foundation, and is reproduced by permission.

Many of these reports come from the United States, but some of the most insightful come from other countries. None calls for full legalization of drugs or views any of the drugs, including marijuana, as harmless, but each of the reports without fail calls for a gentle, humane approach to dealing with drug users and abusers. None of these great commission reports calls for a war on drugs, on users or on addicts. Some countries, notably Great Britain and The Netherlands, have followed much of the advice of these non-partisan expert reports. Others, most notably the United States, have consistently ignored them.

Following are summaries of the key findings of these reports.

Indian Hemp Drugs Commission, *Marijuana*, 1893–94: This 3,281–page, seven-volume classic report on the marijuana problem in India by British and Indian experts concluded: "Viewing the subject generally, it may be added that the moderate use of these drugs is the rule, and that the excessive use is comparatively exceptional. The moderate use produces practically no ill effects." Nothing of significance in the report's conclusions has been proven wrong in the intervening century.

***The Panama Canal Zone Military Investigations*, 1916–1929**: After an exhaustive study of the smoking of marijuana among American soldiers stationed in the zone, the panel of civilian and military experts recommended that "no steps be taken by the Canal Zone authorities to prevent the sale or use of Marihuana." The committee also concluded that "there is no evidence that Marihuana as grown and used [in the Canal Zone] is a 'habit-forming' drug."

Departmental Committee on Morphine and Heroin Addiction, *Report*, 1926 (The Rolleston Report): This landmark study by a distinguished group of British doctors appointed by the government codified existing practices regarding the maintenance of addicts on heroin and morphine by individual doctors and recommended that they continue without police or medical society interference. In coming to this conclusion, these physicians displayed a humane regard for the addicts in their care, perhaps due to their view of the nature of narcotic addiction: "The condition must be regarded as a manifestation of disease and not as a mere form of vicious indulgence." The British addiction experts took pains to state that they did not agree with the opinions of "some eminent physicians, especially in the United States" that addicts "could always be cured by sudden withdrawal."

Mayor's Committee on Marihuana, *The Marihuana Problem in the City of New York*, 1944 (The La Guardia Report): This study is viewed by many experts as the best study of any drug viewed in its social, medical, and legal context. The committee covered thousands of years of the history of marijuana and also made a detailed examination of conditions in New York City. Among its conclusions: "The practice of smoking marihuana does not lead to addiction in the medical sense of the word." And: "The use of marihuana does not lead to morphine or heroin or cocaine addiction, and no effort is made to create a market for those narcotics by stimulating the practice of marihuana smoking." Finally: "The publicity concerning the catastrophic effects of marihuana smoking in New York City is unfounded."

Interdepartmental Committee, *Drug Addiction*, 1961 (The First Brain Report): When the Brain Committee first met at the invitation of the minister of health, its mission was to review the advice given by the Rolleston Committee in 1926. That advice had been to continue to allow doctors to treat addicts with maintenance doses of powerful drugs when the doctors deemed it medically helpful for the patient. Brain I reiterated that advice and in this first report recommended no changes of any significance on the prescribing powers of doctors. This report expanded on one important point alluded to in Rolleston—the authenticity of the existence of "stabilized addicts."

While many American experts doubt their existence, this report explained, "careful scrutiny of the histories of more than a hundred persons classified as addicts reveals that many of them who have been taking small and regular doses for years show little evidence of tolerance and are often leading reasonably satisfactory lives." Six "case histories of known stabilized addicts" were included in an appendix. They were mature, older patients, functioning normally on what would be huge doses of drugs by American standards. "Mr. F.," for example, a clerical worker, was receiving the equivalent of 200 milligrams of morphine tablets each day. It is likely that these patients and their doctors would be dealt with as criminals in the United States.

Joint Committee of the American Bar Association and the American Medical Association on Narcotic Drugs, *Drug Addiction: Crime or Disease?* Interim and Final Reports, 1961: This report was the result of the only major combined study of drug policy made by two of the most important professional societies in the country. Chaired by attorney Rufus King of Washington, D.C., the committee presented a direct challenge to the tough policies of Federal Bureau of Narcotics Director Harry Anslinger, a philosophical ancestor of the previous "drug czar," William Bennett. The blue-ribbon committee included a senior federal judge and was advised by Indiana University's Alfred Lindesmith, one of the most distinguished addiction scholars in history. The report observed, "Drug addiction is primarily a problem for the physician rather than the policeman, and it should not be necessary for anyone to violate the criminal law solely because he is addicted to drugs." The report concluded that drug addiction was a disease, not a crime, that harsh criminal penalties were destructive, that drug prohibition ought to be reexamined, and that experiments should be conducted with British-style maintenance clinics for narcotic addicts.

Interdepartmental Committee, Drug Addiction, *Second Report*, 1965 (The Second Brain Report): Brain II has been consistently misinterpreted by leading American scholars and officials. It did not recommend the dismantling of the British prescription system nor the compulsory registration of addicts, as has been claimed. Instead, Brain II urged that (1) doctors who wished to prescribe "restricted drugs" to addicts for the purpose of maintenance be required to obtain a special license from the Home Office; (2) treatment centers be established for treating addicts who were to be regarded as sick and not criminal; and (3) doctors and other medical personnel be mandated to "notify" the Home Office when they encountered an addict in the course of their professional work. Originally, the category of restricted drugs included heroin and cocaine; now, dipipanone has been added.

The core of the British system remains, however, and in recent years has been reinvigorated. Approximately 200 doctors with special licenses are free to prescribe all drugs, including the restricted medicines, for maintenance of addicts. Also, any doctor, unlike those in the U.S., may prescribe all of the other drugs for maintenance, including, for example, injectable morphine and methadone. Brain II in the end was aimed at controlling a few overprescribing doctors, not at adopting the American system of treating addicts as the enemy.

Advisory Committee on Drug Dependence, *Cannabis*, 1968 (The Wooten Report): This study report on marijuana and hashish was prepared by a group that included some of the leading drug abuse experts of the United Kingdom. These impartial experts worked as a subcommittee under the lead of Baroness Wooten of Abinger. The basic tone and substantive conclusions were similar to all of the other great commission reports. The Wooten group specifically endorsed the conclusions of the Indian Hemp Drugs Commission and the La Guardia Committee. Typical findings included the following: (1) "There is no evidence that in Western society serious physical dangers are directly associated with the smoking of cannabis." (2) "It can clearly be argued on the world picture that cannabis use does not lead to heroin addiction." (3) "The evidence of a link with violent crime is far stronger with alcohol than with the smoking of cannabis." (4) "There is no evidence that this activity . . . is producing in otherwise normal people conditions of dependence or psychosis, requiring medical treatment."

Canadian Government's Commission of Inquiry, *The Non-Medical Use of Drugs, Interim Report,* 1970 (The Le Dain Report): The distinguished Canadian experts on this governmental commission were led by law school dean, later Supreme Court Justice, Gerald Le Dain. The report was similar to the other great commission reports in terms of its non-martial, calm approach to the facts and in its belief that marijuana use did not constitute a great threat to the public welfare. The official governmental commission was remarkable in the extent to which its report portrayed casual drug users as decent, thoughtful citizens whose views deserved the fullest possible hearing by the government in the process of developing drug control strategies.

A mother of four and school teacher was quoted in the report as saying: "When I smoke grass I do it in the same social way that I take a glass of wine at dinner or have a drink at a party. I do not feel that is one of the great and beautiful experiences of my life; I simply feel that it is pleasant, and I think it ought to be legalized." The commission did not ask for that change immediately but instead recommended that serious consideration be given to legalization of personal possession in the near future. The report also urged that police and prosecutors go easy on casual users and keep them out of jail as often as possible.

National Commission on Marihuana and Drug Abuse, *Drug Use in America: Problem in Perspective,* 1973: This commission was directed by Raymond P. Shafer, former Republican governor of Pennsylvania, and had four sitting, elected politicians among its eleven members. The commission also had leading addiction scholars among its members and staff and was appointed by President Nixon in the midst of the drug-war hysteria at that time. While the commission supported much existing policy, it produced two reflective reports, this being the final comprehensive document, which recommended research, experimentation, and humane compromise. The first recommendations of the commission were:

"1. Possession of marihuana for personal use would no longer be an offense, but marihuana possessed in public would remain contraband subject to summary seizure and forfeiture.

"2. Casual distribution of small amounts of marihuana for no remuneration, or insignificant remuneration not involving profit, would no longer be an offense."

The Drug Abuse Council, *The Facts About Drug Abuse,* 1980. A 1972 report to the Ford Foundation, "Dealing With Drug Abuse," concluded that current drug policies were unlikely to eliminate or greatly affect drug abuse. This conclusion led to the creation and joint funding by four major foundations of a broadly based, independent, national Drug Abuse Council. The council reviewed and assessed laws, programs, and projects—federal, state, and local, private and governmental—related to use and misuse of psychoactive drugs. In its final report, the council's board of directors offered a set of observations considered central to the process of reaching more consistent, coherent, and responsible approaches to drug use and misuse.

1. Psychoactive substances have been available throughout recorded history and will remain so. To try to eliminate them completely is unrealistic.
2. The use of psychoactive drugs is pervasive, but misuse is much less frequent, and the failure to make the distinction between use and misuse creates the impression that all use is misuse and leads to addiction.
3. There is a clear relationship between drug misuse and pervasive societal ills such as poverty, racial discrimination, and unemployment, and we can expect drug misuse so long as these adverse social conditions exist.
4. The price of an effective strategy to eliminate drug misuse through the criminal law would be perceived by many Americans as too high in terms of invasions of privacy and abrogations of individual liberties.
5. Drug laws and policies attend insufficiently to the problems of people misusing drugs and too much to the properties of drugs themselves, as though the drugs were somehow inherently to blame.
6. Too many Americans have unrealistic expectations about what drug policies and programs can accomplish.
7. We have a regrettable tendency to blame our drug problems on others, failing to recognize that our drug problems are products of our own national experience.

The council's directors then offered a set of suggestions. Principal among them are the following:

1. Treatment for drug dependence should be available chiefly because people need help, rather than as a crime control or behavior control method.
2. There should be a major study of the effects of drug laws and their enforcement on personal decisions to use or not use illicit drugs.
3. Legislative efforts to decriminalize at both state and federal levels the possession of small amounts of marijuana for personal use should continue.
4. The report ends with the recommendation: ". . . that serious consideration be given to the use of state and local option as a means of attempting solutions appropriate in one place but not in others. Local options could encourage greater flexibility and ingenuity rather than reliance on an unrealistic, rigid homogeneity in national drug policy. We need to respond to the diversity of people who use and misuse drugs, base all our policies on a consistent set of principles seeking to discourage misuse, and keep our seemingly innate

drug-using behavior within reasonable limits through means which do not themselves produce more harm than they prevent.

National Research Council of the National Academy of Sciences, *An Analysis of Marihuana Policy*, 1982. The NAS Committee on Substance Abuse and Habitual Behavior was composed of some of the leading American experts on medicine, addiction treatment, law, business, and public policy. These experts reviewed all of the available evidence on every aspect of the marijuana question. The committee then recommended that the country experiment with a system that would allow states to set up their own methods of controlling marijuana as is now done with alcohol. Under this approach, federal criminal penalties would be removed, and each state could decide to legalize the drug and impose regulations concerning hours of sale, age limits, and taxation.

In the same vein as all the previous major objective studies, this report stated that excessive marijuana use could cause serious harm, that such use was rare, and that, on balance, the current policy of total prohibition was socially and personally destructive. The report placed great emphasis on building up public education and informal social controls, which often have a greater impact on drug abuse than the criminal law. Regarding the possibility of disaster for our youth under legalization, the report observed:

There is reason to believe that widespread uncontrolled use would not occur under regulation. Indeed, regulation might facilitate patterns of controlled use by diminishing the "forbidden fruit" aspect of the drug and perhaps increasing the likelihood that an adolescent would be introduced to the drug through families and friends, who practice moderate use, rather than from their heaviest-using, most drug-involved peers.

Advisory Council on the Misuse of Drugs, *AIDS and Drug Misuse, Part 1*, 1988; *Part 2*, 1989: "The spread of HIV is a greater danger to individual and public health than drug misuse," declared the leading drug abuse and health experts of the United Kingdom who sit on this distinguished quasi-governmental advisory group. This concept operated as the guiding principle in this commission report, one part issued in 1988, another in 1989. In stark contrast to the Bush administration's war plans, the British council provided a comprehensive health plan that seeks to prevent the use of drugs, as is the American goal. However, the plan has realistic goals regarding drug abusers; abstinence in the American mode, where possible, but above all else, health and life. Thus, the Advisory Council accepted the lessons of the "harm reduction" programs of the Liverpool area and recommended that they be spread to the entire United Kingdom. Some of these lessons involve needle exchanges and prescribed drugs for addicts.

The report even went beyond the Liverpool experience when these leading British experts quietly observed, "We believe that there is a place for an expansion of residential facilities where drug misusers may gain better health, skills, and self-confidence whilst in receipt of prescribed drugs." Thus, while the United States is planning more prison space for drug addicts, the United Kingdom is contemplating more hostels where addicts could be taught to live more healthy, more self-confident and more productive lives in the community.

***The Twentieth Annual Report of the California Research Advisory Panel,* 1989**. This panel, appointed by the state legislature of California to regulate all research on controlled substances, reviewed drug policy and recommended that "the legislature act to redirect this state away from the present destructive pathways of drug control." The report noted that we had followed a path of prohibition over the last fifty years and concluded that this policy "has been manifestly unsuccessful in that we are now using more and a greater variety of drugs, legal and illegal." In addition, the failure of prohibition has resulted in "societal overreaction [that] has burdened us with ineffectual, inhumane, and expensive treatment, education and enforcement efforts." They recommended a move toward the formulation of "legislation aiming at regulation and decriminalization" and the winding down of the war on drugs.

The Research Advisory Panel made three specific recommendations for initial legislative action. These were

1. permit the possession of syringes and needles;
2. permit the cultivation of marijuana for personal use; and
3. in order to project an attitude of disapproval of all drug use, take a token action in forbidding the sale or consumption of alcohol in state-supported institutions devoted in part or whole to patient care or educational activity.

The panel recommended immediate and innovative action, concluding it is "incontrovertible that whatever policies we have been following over the past generations must not be continued unexamined and unmodified since our actions to date have favored the development of massive individual and societal problems."

The National Commission of AIDS, "The Twin Epidemics of Substance Use and HIV," July 1991: This indictment of current drug policy focuses on the relationship between the spread of HIV and drug use. The commission criticized the federal government's failure to recognize that these are twin epidemics and found that the "strategy of interdiction and increased prison sentences has done nothing to change the stark statistics" showing spread of AIDS by drug users. The commission singled out the Office of National Drug Control Policy for ignoring AIDS and "neglect[ing] the real public health and treatment measures which could and must be taken to halt the spread."

The commission put forward five recommendations:

1. Expand drug treatment so that all who apply for treatment can be accepted into treatment programs.

2. Remove legal barriers to the purchase and possession of injection equipment.
3. The federal government must take the lead in developing and maintaining programs to prevent HIV transmission related to licit and illicit drugs.
4. Research and epidemiologic studies on the relationships between licit and illicit drug use and HIV transmission should be greatly expanded and funding should be increased, not reduced or merely held constant.
5. All levels of government and the private sector need to mount a serious and sustained attack on the social problems of poverty, homelessness, and lack of medical care that promote licit and illicit drug use in American society.

The National Commission on AIDS could be described as the echo of the British Advisory Council on the misuse of drugs in its report on AIDS and drug misuse, as it made virtually the same policy recommendations. The commission concluded that "the federal government must recognize that HIV and substance use is one of the issues of paramount concern within the 'war on drugs.' Any program which does not deal with the duality of the HIV/drug epidemic is destined to fail." The commission urged the federal government to move away from a law enforcement approach in controlling drugs toward a public health approach, which to date has "been seriously neglected."

Notes

CHAPTER 1

1. "Schultz on Drug Legalization," *Wall Street Journal.*
2. Friedman, "Letter to Bill Bennett."
3. Vallance, but with appreciation of Ogden Nash who wrote of the dandy qualities of candy but contrasted these with the quicker qualities of liquor, and whose heirs and their agents asked too high a price for permission to reproduce the seven-word original.
4. Musto, *American Disease*, Chapter 4.
5. Brecher, *Licit and Illicit Drugs*, 525–26.
6. Goode, *Drugs*, 11–12.
7. P.L. 97–86. Refer to Appendix A for a summary of major federal laws.
8. P.L. 99–570.
9. Gerstein and Harwood, *Treating Drug Problems.*
10. Hughes and Brewin, *Tranquilizng of America.*
11. Helmer, *Drugs*, 1975.
12. Ibid., p. 31.
13. Ibid., p. 5.
14. Williams, *Cocaine Kids.*
15. Miller, *Legalizing Drugs*, Chapter 2.
16. Lusane, *Pipe Dream Blues*, 105.
17. Rice et al., *Economic Costs*, Table 47.
18. Bureau of Justice Statistics, "Drugs and crime facts, 1989."
19. Cited in Bach, *Drug Abuse*, 82.
20. Cited in Perl, "International Aspects."
21. Marshall, *Legalization*, Chapter 3.
22. Bureau of Justice Statistics, "Drugs and crime facts, 1989."
23. Cited in Bach, *Drug Abuse*, Chapter 3.

24. Walters, *Media Briefing.*
25. Kleiman, *Marijuana.*
26. Office of National Drug Control Policy, *What America's Users Spend.*
27. Lusane, *Pipe Dream Blues.*
28. Ibid., 57.
29. Ibid., 50.
30. Hacker, *Two Nations*, 181; See also Morganthau, "Losing Ground."
31. Office of National Drug Control Policy, *National Drug Control Strategy*, 1989.
32. Zimring and Hawkins, *Search.*, 15f.
33. Ibid., 14.
34. Office of National Drug Control Policy, *National Drug Control Strategy*, 1992, 2.
35. Ibid., 36.
36. Ibid., 36.
37. This summary of European drug policies is drawn mainly from a book edited by Albrecht and van Kalmthout, *Drug Policies in Western Europe*, based on a conference sponsored by the Max Planck Institute.
38. Albrecht and van Kalmthout, *Drug Policies*, 79.
39. Ibid., 392.
40. Ibid., 345–46.
41. Ibid., 349.
42. Ibid., 31–34.
43. Decter, "Legitimizing Enslavement."

CHAPTER 2

1. Rice et al., *Economics Costs.*
2. Cited by Ostrowski, "Drug Legalization."
3. Kleiman, *Marijuana.*
4. Air Transport Association, Personal correspondence.
5. Cited by Schuler and McBride, "Notes from the Frontier," 905; See also J. Marshall, "Targeting the Drugs," and J. Marshall, "War on Drugs."
6. Cited by Schuler and McBride, "Notes from the Frontier," 895.
7. Wisotsky, *Breaking the Impasse*, 146.
8. Martin, "Drugs, Crime, and Court Management."
9. Quoted in Alderman and Kennedy, *In Our Defense*, 136.
10. Cited in Ostrowski, "Drug Legalization."
11. Noble, "Testing Employees;" Bullington, "All About Eve," 30.
12. Weeks *v.* United States, 232, U.S. 383, 1914.
13. Mapp *v.* Ohio, 367, U.S. 643.
14. Wisotsky, *Breaking the Impasse*, 124.
15. Sterling, "Bill of Rights."
16. See especially Shannon, *Desperados*; Scott and Marshall, *Cocaine Politics*; McCoy, *The Politics of Heroin: CIA Complicity*; Mabry, "Andean Drug Soldiers"; and Bagley, "Colombia."
17. Reuter, "Drug Interdiction."
18. CIA, *Fact Book 1991.*
19. Shannon, *Desperados*; about Peru, see Gorriti, "Misadventures," and Kirk, "Drug War in Peru."

20. Moody, *An Interview.*

21. Marcus, "Face of Justice." See also "Mass Killings," *New York Times*, which reports some disturbing figures: Nearly 1200 were killed in mainly drug-related incidents in Medellín (Colombia) during January and February 1991. A $4000 bounty on policemen offered by drug cartel leader Manuel Escobar followed by 300 police deaths in Medellín. See also Fazllah, "Cartel."

22. Bagley, "Colombia."

23. Shannon, *Desperados*, p. 415.

24. Ibid., p. 416.

25. Bagley, "Colombia."

26. Shannon, *Desperados*, p. 356. See also Nadelmann, "Latin America and the Drug Trade."

27. Nadelmann, "International Drug Trafficking"; "The DEA in Latin America"; "U.S. Drug Policy"; "Latin America and the Drug Trade."

CHAPTER 3

1. Goldstein and Galant, "Drug Policy."
2. NIDA figures cited in Office of Management and Budget, *U.S. Budget 1992.*
3. NIDA "Capsules" data included with Walters, *Media Briefing*. "Capsules" can be obtained from the National Institute on Drug Abuse Press Office, 5600 Fishers Lane, Rockville, MD 20856.
4. Reuter, "Border"; also Reuter, "Drug Interdiction."
5. Hubbard et al., *Treatment.*
6. Gerstein and Harwood, *Treating Drug Problems.*
7. Hubbard et al., *Treatment*, 156.
8. Ibid., 155.
9. Ibid., p. 160.
10. P.L. 90–351.
11. P.L. 101–647.
12. Martin, "Drugs, Crime, and Court Management."
13. Drugs and Crime Clearinghouse, *Drug Abuse violations*; Treaster, "From the Front Lines."
14. Office of Management and Budget, *U.S. Budget 1992.*
15. Allen et al., *How Drugs Can Affect Your Life.*
16. Ray and Ksir, *Drugs.*
17. P.L. 99–570.
18. P.L. 100–690.
19. Greenhouse, "High Court."
20. McCoy, *Heroin: CIA Complicity.*
21. Sterling, "Bill of Rights."

CHAPTER 4

1. Treaster, "U.S. and Colombia"; Wines, "U.S. and Latin Lands"; and Brooke, "Peru."
2. Reuter, "Drug Interdiction."
3. Ibid. See also Reuter, "Eternal Hope."

4. Cited in Perl, "International Aspects."
5. See Shannon, *Desperados*, Chapter 3, for more details.
6. This conservative estimate is based on information supplied by the Pennsylvania Department of Corrections for constructing security fences in easily accessible locations.
7. Bugliosi, *Drugs in America*, p. 61.
8. This account is based on the analysis by Letwin, "Report from the Front Line."
9. Pichardo, "Viper."
10. Florida, Petitioner *vs.* Terrance Bostick, 111 S. Ct. 2832 (1991).
11. Bazan, "Fourth Amendment."
12. Rusher, "Death Penalty."
13. Letwin, "Report from the Front Line," 816.
14. Jarvik, "Drug Dilemma."
15. Grinspoon, "Psychopharmacological McCarthyism."
16. Lusane, *Pipe Dream Blues*, 105–8.
17. Flynn, *Cocaine*, Chapter 9.
18. Cotts, "The Hard Sell."
19. Lorion and Ross, "Programs for Change." See also the excellent review by Hawkins, Catalana and Miller of research on risk factors in substance abuse in adolescence and early adulthood.
20. Lusane, *Pipe Dream Blues*; Letwin, "Report from the Front Line"; Grinspoon, "Marijuana."
21. Peele, *Diseasing of America.*

CHAPTER 5

1. Trebach, *Great Drug War.*
2. Ibid., 259–65.
3. Ibid., 266–70.
4. Grinspoon, "Marijuana"; "Legalizing Drugs." An earlier review of "Medical uses of illicit drugs" by Grinspoon and James Bakalar also includes the current and potential medical benefits of cocaine, the amphetamines, and the psychedelics. See Chapter 5 in Hamowy, *Dealing with Drugs.*
5. Trebach, *Great Drug War*, 308f.
6. Grinspoon, "Marijuana."
7. E. Marshall, *Legalization.*
8. Bullington, "War or Drug Peace," 15.
9. Single, "Marijuana Decriminalization."
10. Kleiman, *Marijuana.* The same position is argued in his more recent book, *Against Excess.*
11. Trebach and Zeese, *New Frontiers.*
12. See Ostrowski, "Drug Legalization," 670, for an interesting calculation showing that it would take a 1200 percent increase in drug use to produce as many deaths as prohibition causes through murder, AIDS, and poisoned drugs; and asserting that "to prove that prohibition saves more lives than it destroys, it would have to be shown that legalization would result in 6 million *additional* heroin users, and more than 35 million *additional* cocaine users." These statistics are inconceivable when overall trends in legal and illegal drug use are downward.
13. Miller, *Legalizing Drugs*, 143.

14. Hirsch, "Advertising."
15. Posadas *v.* Tourism Company, 478 U.S. 328, 92 L Ed, 106 S CT, 2968, 1986.
16. Summarized in Ostrowski, "Drug Legalization," 637–38.
17. McCoy, *Heroin: CIA Complicity.*

CHAPTER 6

1. Brecher, *Licit and Illicit Drugs*, 528.
2. Summarized in Ostrowski, "Drug Legalization," 647–48.
3. Rice et al., *Economic Costs*, 102, Table 38.
4. Robins, Halzer, and Davis, "Narcotics Use." See also Robins, "Vietnam Drug User."
5. Further summaries of drug use in Vietnam and afterward by Vietnam veterans are contained in Alexander, *Peaceful Measures*; Miller, *Legalizing Drugs*; and Peele, *Diseasing of America*, Chapter 6.
6. Miller, *Legalizing Drugs.* The concept is developed fully in chapter 2.
7. Peele, *Diseasing of America*, 160.
8. Ibid., p. 162.
9. Mabry, "Andean Drug Soldiers," 4.
10. Quoted by Mabry, "Andean Drug Soldiers," 6.
11. Lane, "Newest War."
12. Mabry, "Cops, Robbers, and Soldiers."
13. CIA, *Fact Book 1991.*
14. Ostrowski, "Drug Legalization."
15. Wisotsky, *Breaking the Impasse.*
16. Richards, "Drug Use."
17. Rawls, *Theory of Justice.*
18. Mill, *Utilitarianism*; see also discussion in Wiser, *Political Philosophy*, Chapter 14.
19. Jonas, "Solving the Drug Problem," 761–70, summarizes more than two dozen studies that support the position that the chemical properties of cocaine, heroin, and marijuana are much less harmful to the body than is asserted by conventional wisdom. Some deaths from overdoses of cocaine and heroin have been recorded, but the vast majority of deaths related to those drugs have derived from adulterated impurities and contaminated needles.
20. Wisotsky, *Breaking the Impasse*, Chapter 7, contains an excellent summary of risks to civil rights generated by the drug user.
21. Sirico and Ganssle, *Reason, Comparison, and the Drug War.*
22. Rice et al., *Economic Costs*, 118, Table 47.
23. Quayle interview, C-SPAN, January 13, 1992.
24. Miller, *Legalizing Drugs*, 75.
25. Wisotsky, *Breaking the Impasse*, Chapter 7.
26. Johnson, *America's War.*
27. "Drug-Tough School," *New York Times.*
28. Johnson, *America's War.*
29. Epstein, *Agency of Fear*, 44.
30. Jonas, "Solving the Drug Problem," 783.
31. Karel, "Legalization Proposal."

CHAPTER 7

1. Helmer, *Drugs and Minority Oppression.*

2. Lusane, *Pipe Dream Blues.*

3. See Kyvig, *National Prohibition*; and Kyvig, *Law, Alcohol, and Order.*

4. Galiber, "A Bill to Repeal Criminal Drug Laws."

5. Benjamin and Miller, *Undoing Drugs*, Chapter 11.

6. Tribe, *Constitutional Law*, 479–511.

7. Ibid., 497; referring to Florida Lime and Avocado Growers *v.* Paul, 373 U.S. 132, 142 (1963).

8. Benjamin and Miller, *Undoing Drugs*, 267f.

9. Flynn, *Cocaine*, Chapter 9.

10. See also the review of Grinspoon and Bakalar, "Medical uses of illicit drugs," Chapter 5 in Hamowy, *Dealing with Drugs.*

11. Evans, "Many Forms of Legalization."

12. Miller, *Legalizing Drugs*, 152f. In 1988 the governing council of the American Public Health Association adopted a policy statement that criticized the strategies and misplaced priorities of war on drugs, recommended higher priorities for prevention, treatment and research, and emphasized the importance of using scientific bases for policy formation. In January of 1992 the AFL-CIO convened a meeting of representatives of more than fifty organizations, many of them not conspicuously associated with drug policy reform (e.g., American Hospital Association, American Nurses Association, March of Dimes), which endorsed the release of a critique of the war on drugs, calling it a failure and a fantasy because of its view of drugs as a moral failure rather than a public health problem. These actions and other implications of a public health orientation to drug policy are described in Lewis, "Medical and Health Perspectives."

Sources

BOOKS

Albrecht, Hans-Jorg, and Anton van Kalmthout, eds. *Drug Policies in Western Europe*. Freiburg: Max Planck Institute, 1989.

Alderman, Ellen, and Caroline Kennedy. *In Our Defense: The Bill of Rights in Action*. New York: William Morrow, 1991.

Alexander, Bruce K. *Peaceful Measures—Canada's Way out of the "War on Drugs."* Toronto: University of Toronto Press, 1990.

Allen, William, Nicholas Piccone, and Christopher D'Amanda. *How Drugs Can Affect Your Life*. Springfield: Charles C. Thomas, 1992.

Anderson, Patrick. *High in America*. New York: The Viking Press, 1981.

Bach, Julie. *Drug Abuse*. St. Paul: Greenhaven Press, 1988.

Benjamin, Daniel K., and Roger L. Miller. *Undoing Drugs—Beyond Legalization*. New York: Basic Books, 1991.

Bourne, Peter, ed. *Addiction*. New York: Academic Press, 1974.

Brecher, Edward M. *Licit and Illicit Drugs*. Boston: Little Brown, 1972.

Bugliosi, Vincent T. *Drugs in America: A Citizen's Call to Action*. New York: Knightsbridge Press, 1991.

Drug Abuse Council. *The Facts About Drug Abuse*. New York: The Free Press, 1980.

Duster, Troy. *The Legislation of Morality*. New York: The Free Press, 1970.

Epstein, Edward J. *Agency of Fear: Opiates and Political Power in America*. New York: Putnam's, 1977.

Erickson, Patricia. *Cannabis Criminals—The Social Effects of Punishment on Drug Users*. Toronto: Addiction Research Foundation, 1980.

Flynn, John C. *Cocaine*. New York: Carol Publishing Group, 1991.

Gerstein, Dean, and H. Harwood, eds. *Treating Drug Problems*. Institute of Medicine, Washington, D.C.: National Academy Press, 1990.

Glantz, Meyer, and Roy Pickens, eds. *Vulnerability to Drug Abuse*. Washington, D.C.: American Psychological Association, 1992.

Goode, Erich, *Marijuana*. New York: Atherton Press, 1969.

———. *Drugs in American Society*. New York: Alfred A. Knopf, 1972.

Grinspoon, Lester, and James Bakalar. *Cocaine—A Drug and Its Social Evolution*. rev. ed. New York: Basic Books, 1985.

Hacker, Andrew. *Two Nations: Black, White, Separate, Hostile, Unequal*. New York: Charles Scribner's Sons, 1992.

Hamowy, Ronald. *Dealing with Drugs: Consequences of Government Control*. San Francisco: Pacific Research Institute for Public Policy, 1987.

Helmer, John. *Drugs and Minority Oppression*. New York: The Seabury Press, 1975.

Hubbard, Robert, M. Marsden, J. Rachal, H. Harwood, E. Cavanaugh, and H. Ginzburg. *Drug Abuse Treatment*. Chapel Hill: University of North Carolina Press, 1989.

Hughes, R. and R. Brewin. *The Tranquilizing of America*. New York: Harcourt Brace Jovanovich, 1979.

Inciardi, James A., ed. *The Drug Legalization Debate*. Newbury Park, Cal.: Sage Publications, 1991.

Johnson, Joan L. *America's War on Drugs*. New York: Franklin Watts, 1990.

King, Rufus. *The Drug Hang-up*. New York: Norton, 1972.

Kleiman, Mark. *Marijuana: Costs of Abuse, Costs of Control*. New York: Greenwood Press, 1989.

———. *Against Excess: Drug Policy for Results*. New York: Basic Books, 1992.

Kozel, Nicholas, and Edgar Adams. *Cocaine Use in America: Epidemiologic and Clinical Perspectives*. National Institute on Drug Abuse, Research Monograph 61, 1985.

Kyvig, David. *Repealing National Prohibition*. Chicago: University of Chicago Press, 1979.

———, ed. *Law, Alcohol, and Order: Perspectives on National Prohibition*. Westport, Conn.: Greenwood Press, 1985.

Lindesmith, Alfred R. *The Addict and the Law*. Bloomington: Indiana University Press, 1965.

———. *Addiction and Opiates*. Chicago: Aldine, 1968.

Lusane, Clarence. *Pipe Dream Blues: Racism and the War on Drugs*. Boston: South End Press, 1991.

Marshall, Eliot. *Legalization: A Debate*. New York: Chelsea House, 1988.

McCoy, Alfred W. *The Politics of Heroin in Southeast Asia*. New York: Harper & Row, 1972.

———. *The Politics of Heroin: CIA Complicity in the Global Drug Trade*. Brooklyn: Lawrence Hill Books, 1991.

Mill, John Stuart. *Utilitarianism*. Oxford: Blackwell, 1949.

Miller, Richard L. *The Case for Legalizing Drugs*. New York: Praeger, 1991.

Musto, David F. *The American Disease: Origins of Narcotic Control*. New Haven: Yale University Press, 1973.

Peele, Stanton, *Diseasing of America: Addiction Treatment Out of Control*. Lexington: D.C. Heath, 1989.

Ray, Oakley, and Charles Ksir. *Drugs, Society, and Human Behavior*. 5th Edition. St. Louis Times Mirror/College Publishing, 1990.

Rawls, John. *A Theory of Justice*. Cambridge: Harvard University Press, 1971.

Scott, Peter Dale, and Jonathan Marshall. *Cocaine Politics: Drugs, Armies, and the CIA in Central America*. Berkeley: University of California Press, 1991.

Shannon, Elaine. *Desperados—Latin Drug Lords, U.S. Lawmen, and the War America Can't Win*. New York: Viking, 1988.

Sirico, Robert, and Joseph Ganssle. *Reason, Comparison, and the Drug War: A Statement by Religious Men and Women*. Washington, D.C.: The Religious Coalition for a Moral Drug Policy, 1990.

Stefoff, Rebecca. *The Drug Enforcement Administration*. New York: Chelsea House, 1989.

Szasz, Thomas. *Ceremonial Chemistry*. Garden City: Anchor Press/Doubleday, 1974.

———. *Our Right to Drugs: The Case for a Free Market*. New York: Praeger, 1992.

Trebach, Arnold S. *The Heroin Solution*. New Haven: Yale University Press, 1982.

———. *The Great War, and Radical Proposals That Could Make America Safe Again*. New York: Macmillan, 1987.

Trebach, Arnold S., and Kevin Zeese. *The Great Issues of Drug Policy*. Washington, D.C.: The Drug Policy Foundation, 1990.

———. *New Frontiers in Drug Policy*. Washington, D.C.: The Drug Policy Foundation, 1991.

———. *Strategies for Change*. Washington, D.C.: The Drug Policy Foundation Press, 1992.

Tribe, Laurence H. *American Constitutional Law*. 2d ed. Westbury, N.Y.: The Foundation Press, 1988.

Williams, Terry. *The Cocaine Kids*. New York: Addison Wesley, 1989.

Wiser, James L. *Political Philosophy: A History of the Search for Order*. Englewood Cliffs, N.J.: Prentice Hall, 1983.

Wisotsky, Steven. *Breaking the Impasse in the War on Drugs*. Westport, Conn.: Greenwood Press, 1986.

Zimring, Franklin, and Gordon Hawkins. *The Search for Rational Drug Policy*. New York: Cambridge University Press, 1992.

ARTICLES

"A Symposium on Drug Decriminalization." *Hofstra Law Review* 18, no. 3 (Spring 1990). Hempstead, N.Y.: Hofstra University.

Bagley, Bruce. "Colombia and the War on Drugs." *Foreign Affairs* 67, no. 1 (Fall 1988).

Bazan, Elizabeth. "Changing Contours of the Fourth Amendment." *CRS Review* (September 1991): 19–21. Congressional Research Service.

Beck, Joan. "American Demand Is at the Heart of the Cocaine Plague." *Chicago Tribune*, September 7, 1989.

Brooke, James. "Cali, the 'Quiet' Drug Cartel, Profits from Accommodation." *New York Times*, July 14, 1991.

———. "Peru Develops Plan to Work with U.S. to Combat Drugs." *New York Times*, January 25, 1992.

Bullington, Bruce. "War on Drugs or Drug Peace: A Comparison of American and Dutch Policies." Unpublished manuscript. The Pennsylvania State University, 1991a.

———. "All About Eve. The Many Faces of United States Drug Policy." Unpublished manuscript. The Pennsylvania State University, 1991b.

Burns, Diane H. "Impossible. Finding How Many Use Drugs Casually." *Orlando Florida Sentinel*, October 28, 1989.

Cavanaugh, Suzanne. "Drugs and Crime." *CRS Review* (November-December, 1989): 6–8. Congressional Research Service.

Cotts, Cynthia. "The Hard Sell in the Drug War." *The Nation* (March 9, 1992): 300–302.

Decter, Midge. "Legitimizing Enslavement Will Not Reduce Its Harm." *Washington Post*, March 12, 1990, B11.

DeParle, Jason. "Suffering in the Cities Persists as U.S. Fights Other Battles." *New York Times*, January 27, 1991.

"Drug-Tough School Suspends Students for Sharing Tylenol." *New York Times*, March 1, 1992.

Evans, Richard M. "The Many Forms of Legalization—Beyond 'Whether' to 'How'." In *The Great Issues of Drug Policy*, edited by Arnold Trebach and Kevin Zeese. Washington, D.C.: The Drug Policy Foundation, 1990.

Fazollah, Mark. "Cartel Sets Colombia's Peace Terms." *Centre Daily Times* (State College, Pennsylvania), December 12, 1990.

Friedman, Milton. "An Open Letter to Bill Bennett." *Wall Street Journal*, September 7, 1989.

Galiber, Joseph L. "A Bill to Repeal Criminal Drug Laws: Replacing Prohibition with Regulation." *Hofstra Law Review*, 18, no. 3 (1990): 831–80.

Goldstein, Avram, and Harold Galant. "Drug Policy: Striking the Right Balance." *Science* (September 28, 1990): 1513–21.

Gordon, Diana. "Europe's Kinder, Gentler Approach." *The Nation* (February 4, 1991).

Gorriti, Gustavo. "Misadventures in Cocaland." *New York Times*, September 8, 1991.

Graf, Joseph. "Centre County has Warrant to Seize Marijuana Grower's Home." *Centre Daily Times*, January 16, 1992.

Greenhouse, Linda. "High Court Backs Seizing Foreigners for Trial in U.S." *New York Times*, June 16, 1992.

Grinspoon, Lester. "Marijuana." In *Altered States of Awareness*. San Francisco: W. H. Freeman, 1972.

———. "Psychopharmacological McCarthyism." *The Drug Policy Letter* 2, no. 4 (1990): 6–9.

———. "Legalizing Drugs for Medical Purposes." In *New Frontiers in Drug Policy*, edited by Arnold Trebach and Kevin Zeese. Washington, D.C.: The Drug Policy Foundation, 1991.

Hawkins, David, Richard Catalano, and Janet Miller. "Risk and Protective Factors for Alcohol and Other Drug Problems in Adolescence and Early Adulthood: Implications for Substance Abuse Prevention." *Psychological Bulletin* 112, no. 1 (1991): 64–105.

Hirsh, Peter. "Advertising and the First Amendment." In *New Frontiers in Drug Policy*, edited by Trebach and Zeese.

Hogan, Harry and Charles Doyle. "The Federal Response: A Growing Role." *CRS Review* (November-December 1989): 11–13. Congressional Research Service.

Hollister, Leo E. "Health Aspects of Cannabis." *Pharmacological Reviews* 38, 1 (1986): 1–18.

Inciardi, James, and Duane McBride. "The Case Against Legalization." In *The Drug Legalization Debate*, edited by James A. Inciardi. Newbury Park: Sage Publications, 1991.

Inter-American Commission on Drug Policy. "Seizing Opportunities." Institute of the Americas–University of California, San Diego, June 1991.

Javik, Murray E. "The Drug Dilemma: Manipulating the Demand." *Science* 250, 387 (1990).

Jonas, Steven. "Solving the Drug Problem: A Public Health Approach to Reduction and Use of Legal and Illegal Recreational Drugs." *Hofstra Law Review* 18, no. 3 (1990): 751–94.

Kaplan, John. "Taking Drugs Seriously." *The Public Interest*, no. 92 (Summer 1988): 32–50.

Karel, Richard B. "A Model Legalization Proposal." In *The Drug Legalization Debate*, edited by Inciardi.

Kauffman, Bill. "Do Not Use Military Intervention in the War on Drugs." In *Drug Abuse*, by Julie Bach. St. Paul: Greenhaven Press, 1988.

Kirk, Robin. "Oh! What a Lovely Drug War in Peru." *The Nation* (September 30, 1991).

Kleiman, Mark, and Aaron Saiger. "Drug Legalization: The Importance of Asking the Right Question." *Hofstra Law Review* 18, 703 (1990): 527–67.

Lane, Charles. "The Newest War." *Newsweek*, January 6, 1992.

Larmer, Brook. "The Gateway to Heaven." *Newsweek*, January 20, 1992.

Lawn, John C. "The Issue of Legalizing Illicit Drugs." *Hofstra Law Review*, 18, no. 3 (1990): 703–15.

Letwin, Michael Z. "Report from the Front Line: The Bennett Plan, Street-Level Drug Enforcement in New York City." *Hofstra Law Review* 18, no. 3 (1990): 795–830.

Levine, Michael. "The Drug War, Fight It at Home." *New York Times*, February 16, 1992.

Lewis, David. "Medical and Health Perspectives on a Failing US Drug Policy." *Daedalus* (Summer, 1992): 165–194.

Lorion, Raymond, and James Ross. "Programs for Change: A Realistic Look at the Nation's Potential for Preventing Substance Involvement Among High-Risk Youth." *Journal of Community Psychology, OSAP Special Issue* (1992): 3–9.

Mabry, Donald J. "Cops, Robbers, and Soldiers in the Andes." North-South Center Conference on U.S.–Latin American Relations, Miami, Florida, June 14, 1991.

———. "Andean Drug Soldiers: The Folly Continues." Paper at Fifth International Conference on Drug Policy Reform. Drug Policy Foundation, Washington, D.C. November 1991.

Marcus, David L. "Colombia Alters the Face of Justice Taking Away Faces." State College, Pennsylvania, *Centre Daily Times*, June 18, 1991.

Marquis, John C. (Father), S.T. "Drug Laws are Immoral." *U.S. Catholic*, May 1990.

Marshall, Jonathan. "How our War on Drugs Shattered the Cities." *Washington Post*, May 17, 1992.

———. "Targeting the Drugs, Wounding the Cities." *Washington Post Weekly Edition*, May 25–31, 1992.

Martin, John. "Drugs, Crime, and Urban Trial Court Management: The Unfortunate Consequences of the War on Drugs." *Yale Law Review* 8, no. 75 (1990): 117–45.

"Mass Killings Worsen in Colombia Drug War." *New York Times*, March 3, 1991.

McVay, Douglas. "Marijuana Legalization—The Time Is Now" *The Drug Legalization Debate*, edited by Inciardi.

Moody, John. "A Day with the Chess Player." *Time*, July 1, 1990.

Moore, Mark. "Drugs—Getting a Fix on the Problem and the Solution." *Yale Law and Policy Review*, 8, no. 8 (1990).

Morganthau, Tom. "Losing Ground." *Newsweek*, April 6, 1992.

———. "El Padrino Cuts a Deal." *Newsweek*, June 10, 1991.

Musto, David. "Opium, Cocaine and Marijuana in American History." *Scientific American* (July 1991): 40.

Nadelmann, Ethan A. "The Case for Legalization." *The Public Interest*, no. 92 (Summer 1988): 3–31.

———. "International Drug Trafficking and U.S. Foreign Policy." *The Washington Quarterly* (Fall 1985): 87–104.

———. "The DEA in Latin America: Dealing with Institutionalized Corruption." *Journal of Interamerican Studies and World Affairs* (Winter 1987–88): 2–39.

———. "U.S. Drug Policy: A Bad Export." *Foreign Policy* (Spring 1988): 83–108.

———. "Latin America and the Drug Trade." *Britannica Book of the Year*, 1989.

Nash, Nathaniel C. "Fjuimori Talks Tough But the Coca Thrives." *New York Times*, April 26, 1992.

"National Drug Reform Strategy," Washington, D.C., The Drug Policy Foundation, February, 1992.

National Organization for Reform of Marijuana Laws. "Hemp—It's Not Just Marijuana." Washington, D.C., undated.

Noble, Barbara. "Testing Employees for Drugs." *New York Times*, April 12, 1992.

O'Connell, Lorraine. "Psychologist Challenges Belief About Compulsions." *Orlando Sentinel*. Reprinted in *Centre Daily Times*, January 16, 1992.

Ostrowski, James. "The Moral and Practical Case for Drug Legalization." *Hofstra Law Review* 18, no. 3 (Spring 1990).

Perl, Raphael F. "International Aspects of U.S. Drug-Control Efforts." *CRS Review* (November-December, 1989): 17–19. Congressional Research Service Review.

Pichardo, Nelson A. "Viper at the Door." In *New Frontiers in Drug Policy*, edited by Trebach and Zeese.

Reuter, Peter. "Eternal Hope—America's Quest for Narcotics Control." *The Public Interest* 79 (1985): 79–95.

———. "Can the Border be Sealed?" *The Public Interest*, no. 92 (Summer 1988): 51–65, 232–52.

———. "Quantity Illusions and Paradoxes of Drug Interdiction: Federal Intervention into Vice Policy." *Law and Contemporary Problems* 51, no. 1 (Winter 1988).

Reuter, Peter, J. MacCoun, and Patrick Murphy. *Money for Crime: A Study of the Economics of Crime in Washington, D.C.* Washington, D.C.: The Rand Cooperation, 1990.

Richards, David A. J. "Drug Use and the Rights of the Person—A Moral Argument for Decriminalization of Certain Forms of Drug Use." *Rutgers Law Review* 33 (1981): 607–86.

Roberts, Thomas B. "When the Drug War Hits the Fan." *The Phi Delta Kappan* (September 1991): 58–61.

Robins, Lee, J. Halzer, and D. Davis. "Narcotics Use in Southeast Asia and Afterwards: An Interview Study of 898 Vietnam Returnees." *Archives of General Psychiatry* 32 (1975): 955–61.

Rosenbaum, Marsha. "Just Say What? An Alternative View on Solving America's Drug Problem." *National Council on Crime and Delinquency*, San Francisco, 1989.

Rusher, William. "Death Penalty for Drug Dealers." *Washington Times*, May 19, 1988, 4.

Schmoke, Kurt L. "An Agrument in Favor of Decriminalization." *Hofstra Law Review*, vol. 18, no. 3, 1990, pp. 501–526.

"Scholar Calls for Regulation, Not Legalization." *The Addict Advocate 1*, 1 (Winter 1991–1992): 6.

Schuler, John, and Arthur McBride. "Notes from the Frontier: A Dissident Law Enforcement Perspective on Drug Prohibition." *Hofstra Law Review* 18, no. 3 (1990): 893–942.

"Schultz on Drug Legalization." *Wall Street Journal*, October 27, 1989.

Single, Eric W. "The Impact of Marijuana Decriminalization." Canadian Centre on Substance Abuse, University of Toronto, 1991.

Skolnick, Jerome. "A Critical Look at the National Drug Control Strategy." *Yale Law and Policy Review*, 8, 36 (1990).

Sterling, Eric E. "The Bill of Rights—A Casualty of the War on Drugs." *Vital Speeches of the Day 57*, no. 2 (November 1, 1990).

———. "What Should We Do About Drugs?" *Vital Speeches of the Day 57*, no. 20 (August 1, 1991).

Sweet, Robert W. "Federal Judge Calls for Legalization of Illicit Drugs." *Drug Law Report* 2, no. 13 (January–February 1990).

Treaster, Joseph. "From the Front Lines of the War on Drugs, a Few Small Victories." *New York Times*, February 24, 1991.

———. "U.S. and Colombia Expand Police's Role in Drug Battle." *New York Times*, February 27, 1992.

"Twelve Reasons to Legalize Drugs." *The Pragmatist*, August 1988.

van Vliet, Henk J. "The Uneasy Decriminalization: A Perspective on Dutch Drug Policy." *Hofstra Law Review* 18, no. 3 (Spring 1990), 717–750.

Wenner, Jann S. "Drug War—A New Vietnam?" *New York Times*, June 23, 1990.

Wilson, James Q. "Against the Legalization of Drugs." *Commentary* 81 (1990), 21–28.

Wines, Michael. "U.S. and Latin Lands Plan Drug Fight." *New York Times*, February 28, 1992.

Wisotsky, Steven. "Exposing the War on Cocaine—The Futility and Destructiveness of Prohibition." *Wisconsin Law Review* (1983): 1305–1425.

GOVERNMENT PUBLICATIONS

Bureau of International Narcotics Matters, Department of State. *International Narcotics Control Strategy Report*, March 1991.

Bureau of Justice Statistics. *Report to the Nation on Crime and Justice* 51. Washington, D.C.: U.S. Department of Justice, 1988.

———. *Drugs and Crime Facts, 1989*. Washington, D.C.: U.S. Department of Justice, 1989.

Central Intelligence Agency (CIA). *The World Fact Book 1991*. Washington, D.C.: U.S. Government Printing Office, 1991.

Drug Enforcement Administration. *Illegal Drug Price/Purity Report, Calendar Year 1987–1990*. DEA Office of Intelligence, March 1991.

———. U.S. Department of Justice. *Intelligence Trends* 17, no. 1 (1990).

Drugs and Crime Clearinghouse. *Drug Abuse Violations and Total Estimated Arrests from 1980–1990*. Washington, D.C.: U.S. Department of Justice, August 1991.

Community Epidemiology Work Group. *Epidemiology of Drug Abuse in the United States and Europe*. Rockville, Md.: National Institute on Drug Abuse, June 1988.

National Institute on Drug Abuse (NIDA). *The National Household Survey on Drug Abuse 1990*. Bethesda, Md.: NIDA.

Office of Management and Budget (OMB). *The United States Budget for Fiscal Year 1992*. Washington, D.C.: U.S. Government Printing Office, 1991.

———. *The United States Budget for Fiscal Year 1993*. Washington, D.C.: U.S. Government Printing Office, 1992.

Office of National Drug Control Policy. *National Drug Control Strategy.* Washington, D.C.: U.S. Government Printing Office, 1989.

———. *Guide for State Legislation: Building a Drug-Free Work Force*. Washington, D.C.: U.S. Government Printing Office, 1990.

———. *What America's Users Spend on Illegal Drugs*. Technical Paper, Washington, D.C., June 1991.

———. *National Drug Control Strategy.* The White House, U.S. Government Printing Office, 1992.

Rice, Dorothy, S. Kelman, L. Miller, and Dunmeyer. *The Economic Costs of Alcohol and Drug Abuse and Mental Illness, 1985*. Washington, D.C.: U.S. Department of Health and Human Services, Alcohol, Drug Abuse and Mental Health Administration, 1990.

Robins, Lee. *"The Vietnam Drug User Returns."* Washington, D.C.: U.S. Government Printing Office, 1973.

Snell, Tracey. *"Drug-Related Homicides 1980–1990."* U.S. Department of Justice, Drugs and Crime Data Center and Clearinghouse, September 1990.

Sullivan, Louis W. Press Conference to Release the National Household Survey on Drug Abuse. Washington, D.C.: The White House, December 19, 1990.

Walters, John P. Media Briefing on Household Survey on Drug Abuse and Emergency Room Data from the DAWN (Drug Abuse Warning Network). Washington, D.C.: Office of National Drug Control Policy, December 19, 1990.

U.S. Congress, House. Select Committee on Narcotics Abuse and Control. *Narcotic and Dangerous Drug Control Penalties Under the Controlled Substances Act*, 1990.

———. *Legalization of Illicit Drugs—Impact and Feasibility, part I*. 100th Congress, 2nd session, 1988.

OTHER SOURCES

Electronic Media

Quayle, Danforth. Interview with Robert Woodward, broadcast on Cable-Sponsored Public Affairs Network (C-SPAN), January 13, 1992.

"You're Under Arrest." *60 Minutes*, April 5, 1992.

Court Cases

Florida Lime and Avocado Growers v. Paul. 373 U.S. 132, 142 (1963). Cited in *American Constitutional Law*, by Tribe.

Florida Petitioner *v.* Terrance Bostick, 111 S. Ct. 2382. Decided June 20, 1991.

Mapp *v.* Ohio, 367 U.S. 643; 81 S. Ct. 1684; 6L. Ed. 2 1981 (1961).

Posadas de Puerto Rico Associates *v.* Tourism Company of Puerto Rico, 478 U.S. 328 (1986).

Weeks *v.* United States, 232 U.S. 383, 1914.

Index

About the Author

THEODORE R. VALLANCE is Professor and Associate Dean Emeritus of Human Development at Pennsylvania State University. Earlier, he was chief of planning for the National Institute of Mental Health. He has edited *Values and Ethics in Human Development Professions* (1984) and *Mental Health Services in Transition: A Policy Sourcebook* (1983).